Alexandra Loske

111 Places in Brighton and Lewes That You Shouldn't Miss

T0243648

emons:

Guidebooks for Locals & Experienced Travelers
Join us in uncovering new places around the world at:
www.111places.com

Foreword

At first sight Brighton and Lewes seem like chalk and cheese: Brighton, a buzzing city by the sea with a population of more than 250,000, two universities, a big LGBTQ+ community, and a thriving club and art scene. It has been described as a place 'helping the police with its inquiries', which is partly why it is so vibrant and exciting. By contrast, Lewes, just 15 kilometres east, is a small, seemingly calm town nestled in the folds of the Sussex Downs with a meandering river and a castle ruin, exuding comfortable, middle-class sophistication.

Brighton began life as the fishing village of Brighthelmstone. Without a decent river, and under constant threat of destructive storms and French raids, it is a wonder it survived. Lewes' prospects seemed much better. Located at a strategic point along the navigable River Ouse, it is no surprise William the Conqueror built a castle here in the 11th century. Both towns flourished in the 18th century. The bigger surprise was Brighton, which transformed itself into the most fashionable seaside resort in the country, nicknamed 'London-by-the-Sea'. The flamboyant Prince of Wales, later George IV, built himself the most exotic party palace the country had ever seen, the Royal Pavilion, here. But Lewes knows how to put on a show, too: the Bonfire Night celebrations each November are the largest in the country, and for a few days the town erupts in a frenzy of torch-lit processions and firework displays, attracting tens of thousands of visitors.

I have been living and working in both Brighton and Lewes for more than 25 years, and to me they are connected and complementary. In size, appearance and social make-up they are indeed different, but what they share in bucketloads is a spirit of liberalism and creativity, with a healthy dose of rebelliousness. Visiting both is the perfect introduction to the culture, history and spirit of southern England. This book also introduces places in the greater Brighton area, including Hove, with which Brighton has been a unitary authority since 1997, Shoreham, Falmer and the countryside to the north.

111 Places

1 33 Palmeira Mansions

Sumptuous Victorian splendour

If you think the interior of the Royal Pavilion (see ch. 22) is mind-bogglingly over the top, test your tolerance for extravagance with a trip to nearby Hove, where an elegant building overlooking Palmeira Square is a little-known example of lavish late-19th-century interior design.

Palmeira Mansions, twin blocks of four-storey Italianate houses, were built in 1883–84 to designs by H. J. Lanchester. In 1878, no. 33, on the corner of Church Street and Salisbury Road, was given a higher listed building status (II*) than the others on the grounds of its magnificent interior.

Arthur William Mason, a young and recent widower who had become rich through developing his father's ink manufacturing business, bought the house in 1889. Shortly after he moved in he made some changes to the exterior and transformed the interior completely. Shunning designers, he went entirely with his own taste and desire to show off. The result was an eclectic high-Victorian interior comprising Moorish features, fine furniture, coffered ceilings, embossed wallpaper and all mod cons, including electricity. The grand hallway boasts a marble staircase and is clad in pink alabaster tiles. On the first floor, you find perhaps the most beautiful window in Brighton – an alcove decorated with brightly coloured stained glass. Other gems include a delicate glass overmantel by F & C Osler and hearth tiles by William de Morgan.

Most of the furnishings of the building were sold off in 1941 after Mason's death, but much of the interior has survived. It is now owned by The English Language School and is one of only a few grand 19th-century buildings that has not been divided into flats. Historian Jackie Marsh-Hobbs has researched the building extensively and gives guided tours. All tour proceeds go towards the restoration of the building, predominantly carried out by volunteers.

Address Church Road, BN3 2GB, +44 (0)1273 721771, www.elc-schools.com/about/elc-brighton/palmeira-mansions | **Getting there** 15-minute walk from Hove Railway Station; many buses to Palmeira Square, then 3-minute walk | **Hours** For dates and times of guided tours see website. Private tours can be arranged by email. The building is also usually included in the annual Brighton & Hove Open Door days in May. | **Tip** Look out for the attractive coal hole covers in the pavement outside the house. From here it is just a short stroll down to Hove seafront, past the grandeur of Palmeira Square and Adelaide Crescent.

2 __ Afloat

A hole through which to see the world

Since the early 1990s, Brighton has been commissioning new and exciting public art for the city. Quite a few pieces of recent sculpture are located on or near the seafront. This one, a massive bronze cast of a torus (a geometric shape of a three-dimensional ring) occupies a space between land and sea – at the tip of a groyne (low sea wall) just west of Brighton Pier.

Created in 1998, *Afloat*, endearingly nicknamed 'the donut', was made by Sussex sculptor Hamish Black, who predominantly works on a large scale in steel, bronze, iron and other materials. His work often has strong site-specific and local relevance. He once made a huge sculpture called *Black Blackbird*, created from one of the old elms felled in Brighton by the hurricane of 1987.

Afloat may look like a donut at first sight and, quite appropriately for Brighton, has an air of fun about it, but despite its monumental scale it is a subtle and moving work of art, especially when viewed close up.

The small hole in its centre creates focussed framed views of either land or sea, depending on your vantage point. The piece has acquired a mossy green patina and invites you to touch it. It is often scribbled and graffitied on, but this only adds to its tactile nature. If you look closer you can make out the cut-out shapes of continents adrift on the surface, as well as longitudinal lines radiating from the hole. Afloat was in fact designed by pressing the south and north poles of a globe together to form the shape of a torus. It symbolically links land, sea and sky.

Afloat has a become a popular place for rendezvous, selfies, and even the odd marriage proposal. Most importantly, it is a piece of art that makes us stop in our tracks, laugh or reflect, and look at the world around us in a slightly different way. Try and catch crashing waves in a storm or a glowing sunset sky through that hole.

Address On the groyne c.20 metres west of Brighton Pier, Madeira Drive, BN2 1TW, www.hamishblack.com/afloat | Getting there 5-minute walk from the Royal Pavilion; many bus routes to Old Steine | Hours Always accessible | Tip A few minutes' walk west along the seafront is Passacaglia, a 20-tonne cast-iron abstract sculpture by Charles Hadcock, rising to five metres in height and resembling a large wave or the hull of a ship.

3 — Angel of Peace
A tale of two city-halves

Walk west along the seafront, past the large 19th-century hotels, the West Pier ruin (see ch. 90) and the i360 (see ch. 14) and you see the esplanade opening up into the Hove Lawns, a large green space between the beach and busy Kingsway. You are about to enter Hove, originally a separate development along the Sussex coast, probably, like Brighton, a small fishing village in the Middle Ages. Nowadays it is hard to tell where the border between Brighton and Hove runs, and since 1997 they have been a unitary authority.

Here on the seafront though, there are some clear historic markers of the city's two halves. On the Brighton/Hove border is a tall piece of public sculpture known affectionately as the 'Angel of Peace'. Its official name is *Peace Statue*. It was erected here in 1912 as a monument to King Edward VII, also known as Bertie, who had died in 1910. In his relatively brief reign (1901–10) he became known for his diplomatic skills, acting as a negotiator between several European countries in their disputes, and was called 'the peacemaker'. This statue recognised his efforts and achievements, and was intended as a symbol of hope for continued world peace, commissioned jointly by Brighton and Hove. Sadly, Europe plunged into war just a couple of years later, precisely as Edward had feared.

The bronze statue, designed by Newbury Abbot Trent, is a realistic, large-scale depiction of a beautiful angel standing on a globe, facing the city, her back and enormous wings turned to the sea. She holds symbols of peace in her hands, an orb and an olive branch, the latter raised high above her head. The figure stands on a tall stone pedestal with a three-stepped base, adding to its height and impact. It is a beautiful expression of peace, calm and unity, and looks particularly stunning silhouetted against the early morning sky or at sunset.

Address Kingsway, BN3 2WN | Getting there 20-minute walk from Brighton Railway Station; many buses to Norfolk Square | Hours Always accessible | Tip The outdoor Meeting Place Café just behind the Angel of Peace is a true Brighton (and Hove!) institution. There has been a café here since the 1930s. It serves customers from dawn till dusk and hardy souls can be seen drinking tea here in the fiercest of weather conditions. The kiosk even withstood the hurricane of 1987, as did its customers (themeetingplacecafe.co.uk).

4__Aubrey Beardsley's Birthplace
Master of line and naughtiness

Of all the illustrious people who have a connection with Brighton, the artist Aubrey Beardsley, a contemporary of playwright Oscar Wilde, is perhaps the most notorious, and one of the most interesting. Beardsley was part of the 'Aesthetic Movement', a group of artists and writers in the later 19th century that celebrated beauty, eroticism, and 'art for art's sake'. Unsurprisingly, this came with a heavy dose of decadence and scandal. His largely black-and-white graphic work is clear and elegant, heavily influenced by Japanese aesthetics, combining sinuous lines with unflinchingly sexual motifs. He provided illustrations for works as diverse as Thomas Malory's Le Morte d'Arthur, Aristophanes' *Lysistrata* and Oscar Wilde's play *Salome*. He also worked for popular magazines and was a co-founder of the literary periodical *The Yellow Book*, for which he designed many covers.

This wild child of the art scene was born in Brighton on 21 August, 1872, a stone's throw from Brighton Railway Station (see ch. 13), in the home of his maternal grandfather. The house (and its lovely commemorative plaque to the 'Master of Line') is now 31 Buckingham Road, but was once number 12. Many people assume he was born in a maternity hospital that stood at the other end of Buckingham Road, and miss the actual house. He did, however, have a connection with the hospital, as it was formerly Brighton Grammar School. Young Beardsley attended in the 1880s, and here his talents were first recognised.

Beardsley was an eccentric and provocative artist, keen to shock and shake up Victorian society with erotic and often pornographic images. His association with Oscar Wilde cost him his position at *The Yellow Book*. He was sacked after Wilde was convicted of sodomy in 1895, and his health deteriorated soon after. In March 1898 he died of tuberculosis, aged only 25.

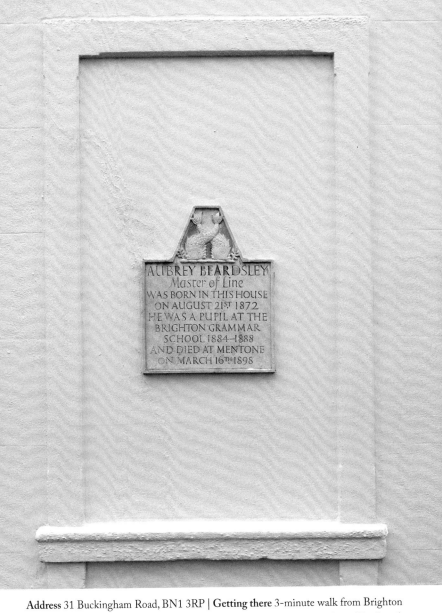

AUBREY BEARDSLEY
Master of Line
WAS BORN IN THIS HOUSE
ON AUGUST 21ST 1872
HE WAS A PUPIL AT THE
BRIGHTON GRAMMAR
SCHOOL 1884–1888
AND DIED AT MENTONE
ON MARCH 16TH 1898

Address 31 Buckingham Road, BN1 3RP | **Getting there** 3-minute walk from Brighton Railway Station; many buses to Brighton Station | **Hours** Not open to the public. Local historian Alexia Lazou regularly offers Beardsley-themed walking tours. Check Brighton events websites for details. | **Tip** Walk up Buckingham Road until you reach Buckingham Place. On the opposite side to your right is the West Hill Tavern, from where you have a panoramic view over the vast railway land behind Brighton Railway Station. The impact of the arrival of the railway on the town suddenly becomes clear.

5 Bandstand

An open cage for birds and humans

Brighton's seafront perhaps looked its most magnificent in the later 19th century, between the arrival of the railway and the invention of motor cars. By the 1880s there were three piers offering entertainment and amusement, the esplanades had been developed and the seafront was lined with grand hotels providing accommodation for thousands of short-stay visitors. Dotted along the seafront of Brighton and Hove were also 12 Victorian bandstands, used for musical performances and a variety of other events. Of these romantic structures only one survived, by the skin of its teeth.

Designed and built by the borough surveyor Philip Lockwood in 1884, the cast-iron structure is one of the most splendid examples of this type of seaside architecture. Its unofficial name is 'the birdcage'. If it does resemble a cage it is one of the most beautiful kind. The main octagonal structure is linked to the upper promenade via a bridge, and it feels a little like leaving solid ground when you walk onto the Bandstand. Despite the heavy materials used creating it, the building emanates lightness, looking suspended. What an experience it must have been listening to music here in the late 19th century.

It was not to last. Performances stopped in the 1960s when 20th-century traffic noise made it impossible to listen to concerts, and for more than 40 years the building was largely neglected and fell into disrepair, like so many other older seaside structures. The bridge was taken down in the 1970s, making the Bandstand inaccessible.

It was rescued thanks to the initiative of residents who campaigned for its restoration. In 2008, Brighton & Hove Council eventually began cleaning and reconstructing it, complete with footbridge, and re-opened it in 2009, with a café at beach level. Now brass bands play here again and the space is licensed for wedding ceremonies.

Address Kings Road (opposite Bedford Square), BN1 2PQ, +44 (0)1273 292712 (Council events office), www.brighton-hove.gov.uk | Getting there 15-minute walk from Brighton Railway Station; nearest bus stop Waitrose in Western Road | Hours Always accessible. For events, music performances in the summer and hire times check the website. | Tip Just a 2-minute walk east of the Bandstand is a recently redeveloped fenced playground area with a large paddling pool for toddlers. If you have small children there is no better place to spend a hot summer day, with easy access to ice cream and coffee from nearby cafés and stalls.

6 Bardsley's

Four generations of fun, fish and chips

Ask Brightonians whether they can name and recommend a traditional fish and chip shop and many will say, without hesitation: Bardsley's. The celebrated chippy has a deservedly good reputation, excellent hygiene ratings, and is fully licensed. You find it in Baker Street, in the London Road area, where day tourists normally don't venture unless they have heard of Bardsley's. Look out for its distinctive black-and-white exterior among a range of traditional independent shops and businesses such as pawn shops, barbers and pet shops, peppered with the odd new and experimental establishment.

Until very recently, Bardsley's belonged to four consecutive generations of the same family. Roy Brown ran it for much of the last 50 years, joined in 1989 by his son Neil, who was then only 14 years old. The shop was founded in 1926 by Roy's wife's grandfather, Ben Bardsley, who is immortalised in a wall mosaic, made by a happy customer, in the main eating area. Originally a blacksmith from Lancashire, Ben was hit by the Great Depression in the 1920s and decided to start a new business here in Brighton. In 1963 the eatery moved to its present location. Since then it has served many locals, international students, and London visitors who have heard of the legendary fish and chip shop where the whole world seems to come together.

All of Bardsley's fish is line-caught, and if you come between January and March, you may be able to taste the rare seasonal Norwegian black cod – it's the only place in the UK where you can do so. There are tales of weddings that have taken place here in the upstairs room, with Champagne flowing and bands playing. And what is the secret of this happy place? At Bardsley's, customers are made to feel special, and this – luckily – hasn't changed under the new owners.

Address 22–23 Baker Street, BN1 4JN, +44 (0)1273 681256, www.bardsleys-fishandchips.co.uk | Getting there 15-minute walk from Brighton or London Road Railway Station; many buses to Open Market | Hours Tue – Sat, lunch noon – 3pm, dinner 4.30 – 9.30pm | Tip Marvel at the fantastical window displays of the Skin Candy tattoo studio at 18 Baker Street, brimming with new-age taxidermy that may inspire your choice of tattoo.

7 __ The Basketmakers Arms

A pub with many secret messages

The Basketmakers is one of those pubs that sounds almost too good to be true: cosy, friendly, in the centre of town but with the feel of a country pub, offering great food, great beer, and a little bit of mystique.

It really does exist. The corner pub is located in a slightly tucked-away part of the bustling North Laine area where baskets were once made (hence the name), but within a short walk of Brighton Railway Station. It has won too many awards to list here, but a few years ago it was deservedly named Brighton Pub of the Year twice in succession, and has Fuller's Master Cellarman status for exceptional cellar standards. You have a choice of eight different ales, premium craft lagers and a selection of dozens of whiskies. The Basketmakers also serves excellent food using high-quality meat from Brighton butchers and seafood caught locally. At weekends you need to get there early or book ahead for the delicious roast lunches.

The walls are decorated with hundreds of vintage tins, in which people have been leaving scribbled notes for many years. Nobody quite knows how or when this tradition began, but cryptic messages, doodles and random photographs are in almost all the tins. Philosophical musings and surreal correspondences between strangers have been found in some of them, such as 'Why have we never met?' answered with 'I have been travelling the world to find you but we keep missing each other. Call me – that's easier…', followed by a phone number. You are of course welcome to add your own when you visit.

The Basketmakers is one of those places you fear might disappear any day, but hopefully it will be there for good. It has a good track record for longevity: the exquisitely named former landlord Blue ran it for 35 years, and it is now in the good hands of Zoe Rogers, who thankfully hasn't changed much about it.

Address 12 Gloucester Road, BN1 4AD, +44 (0)1273 689006, www.basket-makers-brighton.co.uk, bluedowd@hotmail.co.uk | **Getting there** 7-minute walk from Brighton Railway Station; many buses to North Road | **Hours** Mon–Sat 11am–11pm, Sun noon–11pm | **Tip** Walk up Gloucester Road for just a couple of minutes and you will be at the heart of the North Laine area. The pedestrianised Kensington Garden to the left and Sidney Street to the right are the most colourful streets in Brighton, with many quirky independent retailers and cafés.

8_ Beyond Retro

The ethical way to wear jeans, leather and more

Beyond Retro is a small chain offering vintage clothes and accessories. It originated in 2002 as a warehouse-turned-retail store in East London and has since gone from strength to strength. It now has nine stores in the UK and in Sweden and has become one of the most exciting vintage retailers in the country. The company's ethical business model and aesthetic style fits Brighton like a glove, and this treasure trove of highly individual, recycled and upcycled fashion is a joy to behold.

While there is no shortage of vintage clothes shops in Brighton (see ch. 41), in addition to the many charity shops offering good-quality second-hand clothing, Beyond Retro has taken the concept of sustainability and circular economy to another level. The Brighton store is a vast former-garage, and retains an industrial feel. The prominent corner building in the fashionable North Laine invites you to spend hours browsing for the most appealing and interesting pieces.

Beyond Retro employs a professional team of buyers and stylists who source and select the clothes and accessories offered in the shops and online. The shop is highly educational, explaining with snappy graphics how much water is needed to produce a pair of denim trousers. Bringing a child with a blossoming interest in clothes and fashion here may convey a few important messages about the manufacture of clothes. Why buy a new pair of jeans when you can choose from hundreds of recycled ones, and help the environment? The company also makes new things out of old, such as a range of bags and backpacks made from old leather jackets. And if in the colder months you entertain the thought of wearing real fur, the only acceptable way to do so is to buy one of Beyond Retro's simple, stylish hats made from mid-20th-century fur coats. You may still feel slightly guilty, but at least the coats haven't gone into landfill.

Address 23 Gloucester Road, BN1 4AD, +44 (0)20 7729 9001, www.beyondretro.com |
Getting there 10-minute walk from Brighton Railway Station, 5-minute walk from the
Royal Pavilion; many buses to North Road or Old Steine | Hours Mon–Sat 10am–6pm,
Sun 11am–5pm | Tip A two-minute walk away, on the corner of Vine Street and North
Road, is Bill's, a buzzy place that serves simple, delicious food in a large double-height space.
The first Bill's was in Lewes, combining the concepts of café, restaurant and grocery store.
The Brighton branch has a particular urban feel to it.

9 Black Lion Lane

Single-file traffic only in this twitten

A Sussex word for a narrow lane between houses is 'twitten'. First recorded in the 13th century, it may derive from an old German word, 'zwischen', meaning 'in between'. Brighton has many twittens, linking main streets such as East and West Streets, Middle and Ship Streets. Twittens were never wide enough for coaches or carriages and tended to be dark and sometimes dangerous, but they also provided shelter from the elements for their inhabitants. They have triggered many an urban myth and inspired stories in both film and literature. They are sources of great intrigue for visitors, but also shortcuts for locals wanting to avoid busy main streets. One can cover considerable distances in Brighton (not just in the old town) using these alternative routes, but you have to know where they are.

Black Lion Lane in the heart of the Lanes area is the narrowest of these twittens. It links Black Lion Street and Ship Street. Beyond Ship Street it continues as another lane, Ship Street Gardens, leading to Middle Street. Black Lion Lane is so narrow, only one person can pass through it at a time, so one has to negotiate with anyone approaching from the other end.

The entrance from Black Lion Street is flanked by two public houses with fascinating histories. On the right is the Cricketers Arms, said to be on the site of the oldest Brighton pub, possibly dating from 1545. The current building is Victorian and was novelist Graham Greene's favourite haunt. On the left is the Black Lion pub, a reconstruction of the Black Lion Brewery that stood here in the 16th century. It was bought in the 1540s by Deryk Carver, a Flemish Protestant immigrant who grew hemp for his brewery in nearby fields and also ran an inn. Carver was one of the eleven Protestant martyrs arrested under Queen Mary's rule for practising their faith and burnt outside what is now Lewes town hall on 22 July, 1555 (see ch. 105).

Address Between Black Lion Street and Ship Street, BN1 1NL | Getting there 5-minute walk from the Royal Pavilion; many buses to North Street or Old Steine | Hours Always accessible | Tip On the corner opposite The Cricketers and the Black Lion pub is Food for Friends, a much-loved and award-winning vegetarian restaurant that has been serving innovative and delicious food here since 1981 (www.foodforfriends.com).

10__Bom-Bane's

Mechanical hats and musicals with your dinner

It's small, colourful, and possibly the happiest place to have a meal –
and much more. Prepare to be surprised and mesmerised when you
visit the category-defying Bom-Bane's. It is café, restaurant, theatre,
opera, funfair and theme park rolled into a small terrace house just
off the beaten track in central Brighton.

Bom-Bane's was opened in 2006 by musician and poet Jane 'Bom-
Bane', who has a long and illustrious history of collaborations with
many musicians. She writes musicals that are performed in the café,
in conjunction with themed food evenings. A recent one told the
story of the lost Brighton river, Wellesbourne, another traced the
history of the building. There is regular live music and comedy, and
every Wednesday Jane puts on an incredibly good value Screen'n'Supper film night. Films are shown in a magical downstairs space with
a small stage.

Jane often performs original songs and poetry after or during dinner, either on her own or with fellow singers, to the accompaniment
of harmoniums and mechanical hats. When these amazing hats, all
made by Jane, are not being used in performances they form part of
the fantastical decoration of the café. Its walls are plastered with artwork, some created by guests, others by Jane's artist friends, but the
most wonderful objects are Jane's puppets, hats and other objects.
Look out for a miniature version of Jane's former London house,
complete with lighting and a puppet of Jane herself in it.

At Bom-Bane's you find magical worlds within worlds, and you
can have dinner at tables with very special effects. You can choose
from the see-though Tablerone, the TurnTable, which turns very
slowly while you are eating, the Aesop's Table(s) that shows black-
and-white clips of Aesop's fables, the very musical Twenty-Seven
Chimes Table, the Water Table, which features a pier, or the rather
disorientating Uns-Table.

Address 24 George Street, BN2 1RH, +44 (0)1273 606400, bom-banes.com, janebombane@yahoo.co.uk | Getting there 5-minute walk from the Royal Pavilion; many buses to Old Steine or St James's Street | Hours Tue from 6pm if a music night, Wed 12.30–11pm, Thu 5–11pm, Fri 5–11.30pm, Sat 12.30–11.30pm, closed Sun & Mon but available for parties. Check the website for events. | Tip George Street and St James' Street are lined with many independent shops, cafés, bars and clubs. Look out for the moving AIDS Memorial Sculpture by Romany Mark Bruce on the New Steine (BN2 1PA). It forms a shadow in the shape of the red ribbon.

11_Booth Museum
400 windows on natural history's history

Look out for the fire-engine-red wooden doors of this one-storey Victorian brick building halfway up Dyke Road on the way out of Brighton. It's worth getting off the bus and postponing your visit to the Chattri (see ch. 17) or Devil's Dyke (see ch. 19) for a couple of hours, as you will be rewarded with one of the most intriguing museums you have ever seen. You may well think you have travelled back in time 150 years, but the Booth's unspoilt Victorian appearance is bolstered by knowledgeable and dedicated staff and contemporary interactive museum features.

The museum was built in 1874 to house the private collection of the ornithologist Edward Thomas Booth (1840–90). Booth bequeathed his private museum of thousands of specimens of stuffed animals, insects, bones and fossils to the Corporation of Brighton. More than 400 dioramas line the walls: glass cases in which natural habitats of birds and other creatures are recreated to form the right visual context for the stuffed specimen. Although some now show their age, they are important educational tools, allowing visitors to examine the many birds in all their beautiful detail. This is bird-watching in aspic, and wandering past the long rows of glass cases is curiously calming. It is highly probable, though not confirmed, that Booth was the first to create elaborate dioramas in a museum.

For a small museum, the Booth holds an impressive set of records. It has both the largest collection of Central American butterflies and the sixth-largest insect collection in the UK. Look out for curiosities such as the disturbing 'Merman' – a Victorian taxidermy hoax – and marvel at the state-of-the-art contemporary taxidermy work carried out here. Kids can get hands-on with natural history in the interactive Discovery gallery and the museum regularly puts on special themed events.

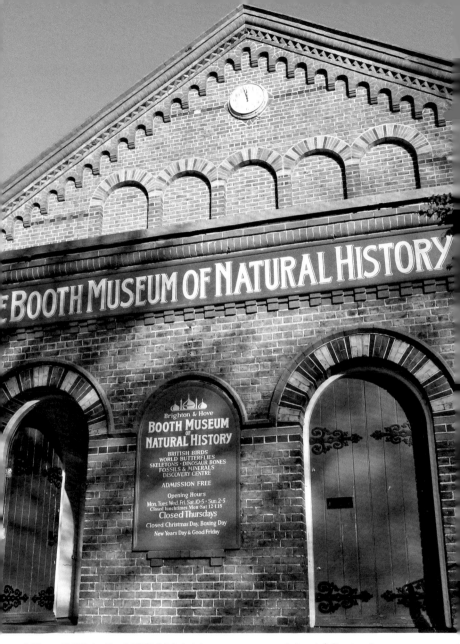

Address 194 Dyke Road, BN1 5AA, brightonmuseums.org.uk/booth | **Getting there**
20-minute walk from Brighton Railway Station; bus 14, 14C, 27, 77 to Booth Museum |
Hours Mon, Tue, Sat & Sun 10am–5pm, Wed (school term time) 2–5pm, Wed (school
holidays) 10am–5pm | **Tip** Across the road is Dyke Road Park, which boasts a children's
playground, a rose garden, tennis courts, an open-air theatre and a small café. From here you
have panoramic views of Brighton and Hove all the way to the sea.

12 Brighton Fishing Museum
The legacy of 'Mr Seafront'

Brighton's seafront between the two piers has been undergoing massive regeneration and reconstruction work in recent years, with more projects in the pipeline. It seems that the council recognises the historical, social and cultural significance of this stretch. It wasn't always so. By the 1980s the seafront looked tired, messy and run-down.

It was largely down to one determined man that we now have the Brighton Fishing Quarter and within it the charming Fishing Museum, located by the Kings Road Arches on the lower esplanade. Andy Durr, who died in 2014, was a Londoner who chose Brighton as his home and for decades raised awareness of its rich seaside heritage, so much so that he was nicknamed 'Mr Seafront'. He was self-educated, deeply political – a Labour councillor and lifelong trade unionist – and in 2000 became mayor of Brighton & Hove.

In the early 1990s he campaigned for the regeneration of the Kings Road Arches area, with the aim of making it a place that brings to life the past and present of Brighton's fishing industry. With great persuasive power he managed to convince the council to invest in the project, and in 1994 the Fishing Museum opened, flanked by premises of actual Brighton fishermen (see ch. 54) and a range of artists' studios and shops.

The museum, run entirely by volunteers and free to visit, tells the story of the fishing community in Brighton through film footage, photography, prints, memorabilia and of course fishing boats and equipment. Durr's passion still shines through the lovingly displayed objects. A permanent exhibition explores swimming culture, Punch and Judy shows, and the sad story of the West Pier (see ch. 90). You can admire pieces of wood and cast iron salvaged after the fires that destroyed it in the early 2000s. It is fair to say that Andy Durr has left a lasting legacy and paved the way for the larger projects happening now.

Address Kings Road Arches, BN1 1NB, +44 (0)1273 723064, www.brightonfishingmuseum.org.uk | Getting there 15-minute walk from Brighton Railway Station; many buses to Churchill Square or Old Steine | Hours Daily, no specific times | Tip If you want to find out more about Brighton's watery history, visit the Images of Brighton gallery on the ground floor of Brighton Museum, which tells Brighton's history from fishing village to liberal city by the sea (brightonmuseums.org.uk/brighton/exhibitions-displays/images-of-brighton).

13 Brighton Railway Station

Mocatta's marvel, much changed

The arrival of the railway changed the way Brighton looked and developed like no prior event, with the possible exception of becoming a fashionable seaside resort in the mid-18th century. This, however, was on a different scale: a comparison of Brighton maps from before and after the opening of the London-to-Brighton railway line shows the dramatic expansion of the town, with many of the new streets and houses being built in the vicinity of railway stations.

At the heart of this was Brighton's main station at the top of Queen's Road, a northward extension of West Street, the medieval western edge of Brighton. Proposals for a railway link between London and Brighton had been made as early as 1823, but it would take until 21 September, 1841 for the first train to leave Brighton for London. The 80-kilometre line had taken three and a half years to build, a project masterminded by Sir John Rennie and John Rastrick (see ch. 48 and 26).

This important new line needed a terminus building reflecting its importance. Early on in the project, the job of designing Brighton Railway Station was given to the Jewish architect David Mocatta, a pupil of Sir John Soane, and one of the first fellows of RIBA (Royal Institute of British Architects). Before Brighton, he had designed several synagogues in London. It wasn't an easy task, as the station building had to be constructed on a massive platform. He rose to the occasion though, designing a two-storey building in the fashionable Italianate style, with an elegant colonnaded arcade on its south side. The bridge over Trafalgar Street was built a few years later to make access easier, and regrettably the colonnade was removed at some point. In the early 1880s, a cast-iron canopy was added to the forecourt, and a gorgeous, sweeping, 182-metre train shed was added at the rear. Both were designed by H. E. Wallis, and partly obscure Mocatta's work.

Address Queens Road, BN1 3XP | **Hours** Open during train service | **Tip** As is often the case with roads near main stations, Queen's Road has always looked a bit rough and unloved, partly due to unsympathetic post-war building projects, but recently the Council has made an effort and this thoroughfare leading to the sea is cleaner and tidier now, and some interesting new cafés and shops have appeared.

14 British Airways i360
Take to the sky in a shiny donut

Not since John Nash's oriental makeover of the Royal Pavilion in 1815 has any Brighton building attracted so much debate, enthusiasm and criticism as the i360. It seems fitting that this slender structure, the country's tallest moving observation tower, opened in 2016, almost exactly 200 years after Nash started adding unflinchingly exotic features to the Prince Regent's palace.

The i360 was conceived by Marks Barfield Architects, who in 1999 gave us the immensely popular London Eye on the banks of the Thames. Here in Brighton they envisaged a 'vertical pier', in a nod to Brighton's historic piers. The tower was built on the beach, on land owned by the West Pier Trust, who some years ago had to shelve plans of rebuilding the Victorian West Pier that stood here. Only a fragment of this survives, detached from the land (see ch. 90).

The idea behind the observation tower was to create something truly spectacular that would become a tourist attraction and a contemporary monument to the spirit of Brighton. Since planning began in 2006, there has been much heated debate about the intrusive and dominating nature of such a tall building. The critics have a point: the i360 has indeed changed the look of the Brighton skyline. Being taller than any other building in the area, it frequently comes into view unexpectedly between houses.

It rises to 168 metres, with a shiny, fully enclosed glass pod, quickly nicknamed 'flying donut', taking up to 200 visitors to a height of 138 metres. During the gentle 20- to 25-minute flights, as the operators call them, you get breath-taking 360-degree views over the sea and the South Downs. On a good day you can see as far as the Isle of Wight in the west and Beachy Head in the east. It is a building typical of Brighton – daring, ambitious, and a bit crazy, but it does feel rather special seeing a storm coming in when you're at the top.

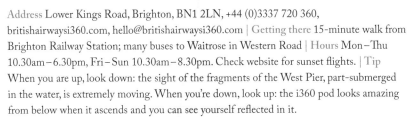

Address Lower Kings Road, Brighton, BN1 2LN, +44 (0)3337 720 360, britishairwaysi360.com, hello@britishairwaysi360.com | Getting there 15-minute walk from Brighton Railway Station; many buses to Waitrose in Western Road | Hours Mon–Thu 10.30am–6.30pm, Fri–Sun 10.30am–8.30pm. Check website for sunset flights. | Tip When you are up, look down: the sight of the fragments of the West Pier, part-submerged in the water, is extremely moving. When you're down, look up: the i360 pod looks amazing from below when it ascends and you can see yourself reflected in it.

15 _ Café Coho, Ship Street
Don't tell anyone about that upstairs room!

Brighton is blessed (some say cursed) with an extremely high number of good independent cafés, perhaps more so than most other British cities. Brighton has indeed turned coffee and café culture into a fine art. There is really no excuse to have anything less than a beautifully crafted cup of coffee in this town. Tourists can even pick up an 'Independent Brighton & Hove Coffee Guide', which reviews more than 30 coffee spots.

For a near-perfect combination of style, delicious food and outstanding coffee, Café Coho deserves to be singled out. The independent café, which describes itself as an espresso bar, was founded in 2010 by James Wilson, whose aim was to serve high-quality coffee and food in a welcoming and friendly space. It has since won awards and now has three branches: Ship Street in the Lanes, Queen's Road near Brighton Railway Station, and a smaller, counter-style version in Churchill Square shopping centre. With high ceilings and exposed brickwork, the Queen's Road branch has a whiff of downtown Manhattan about it, perfect for people-spotting while waiting for the next train.

The Ship Street branch wins the atmosphere prize. The Georgian two-storey townhouse is slightly set back from the main road, right at the heart of the Lanes, only a couple of minutes' walk from the sea. The décor is all warm stripped wood and vintage furniture. The most coveted place is by the bow window in the upstairs room, where you can watch the world go by from an elevated position, while sipping their signature Revelation blend coffee made on La Marzocco machines. In the early days this room was a little-known secret and one could see students, writers and office workers decamping here for hours. Recently, rumours have gone around that it would no longer be allowed to write entire term papers or novels there, to give other people a chance to enjoy the space, and the coffee.

Address 53 Ship Street, BN1 1AF, www.cafecoho.co.uk, info@cafecoho.co.uk | Getting there 10-minute walk from Brighton Railway Station; many buses to North Street | Hours Mon 8am–6.30pm, Tue–Fri 8am–7pm, Sat 9am–8pm, Sun 9am–7pm | Tip The adjoining Union Street leads to the warren of narrow lanes and twittens most associated with the old fishing village. In the 20th century, many jewellers and antiques traders set up shop here. There is still a high density of the former, so you can go for a walk around the area admiring the bling in the windows.

16__Catalyst Club
Passionate spoken words and more

If you fancy some truly passionate and amusing talks on intriguing subjects, in the company of an equally entertaining host and audience, then the Catalyst Club in the basement of the Latest Music Bar is your place. The spoken word event takes place once a month and is organised by writer David Bramwell, whose aim is to make his club 'open to anyone with a passion, no matter how bizarre or niche'.

In the early years of the millennium, Bramwell felt the need to invent a platform for the spoken word that was to be as egalitarian as possible, where people could share their philosophies and quirky areas of expertise. The first Catalyst Club took place in 2004 with talks on the history of the Martini, the writer Max Beerbohm and an American rock band. Since that Martini-infused first evening there have been more than 500 talks, which have included topics such as the Suffragettes, zombies, demonology, and 'sex in classical music' (some of this – the music, not the sex – was performed during the presentation).

The format of the Catalyst Club is simple and effective: for a modest entry fee, the audience gets to hear three 15-minute talks by guest speakers. There is a bit of mystery involved with each club night, as it is not usually known who will speak and which topics will be covered. The age range of the audience is one of the widest you will ever see at a Brighton event, and talks are generally of high quality and genuinely thought-provoking.

The Catalyst Club has turned out to be a catalyst indeed: Bramwell tells stories of several couples who first met at the club, and there have been spin-off events in the form of themed specials as well as the Wellsbourne Club night, where the talks relate to Brighton and its surroundings. The Club has even made it on to a special programme on BBC Radio 4, and podcasts are available on the website.

Address Latest Music Bar, 14–17 Manchester Street, BN2 1TF, +44 (0)1273 687171, latestmusicbar.co.uk, bookings@thelatest.co.uk | **Getting there** 5-minute walk from the Royal Pavilion; many buses to Old Steine or Sea Life Centre | **Hours** Catalyst Club: every 2nd Thursday of the month, 8–10.30pm; for spin-offs and specials, such as the Lewes leg of the Club, see www.catalystclub.co.uk | **Tip** The area around the Latest Music Bar is busy and popular at night. For some exceedingly good, simple Italian food before you head to the Catalyst Club, have an early meal at the nearby VIP Pizza, 19 Old Steine, BN1 1EL.

17 __ Chattri

Solemn tribute to the Indian war dead

High on the Downs, at Brighton's northern border with West Sussex, stands a memorial that has a special significance in Brighton's and India's histories. The Chattri is dedicated to the memory of Indian soldiers who died in Brighton's military hospitals during World War I. It was erected near the spot where, between 1914 and 1915, 53 Sikhs and Hindus were cremated, and also commemorates 19 Muslims who died in Brighton but were buried in Woking.

You may wonder why so many Indian soldiers died in hospitals in Brighton. The Indian Army played a vital role in World War I. In the early months of the war it provided large numbers of troops, who fought at the Western Front for the British cause. From 1914 to 1916 the Royal Pavilion Estate and its historic buildings, which had been in municipal ownership since 1850, were turned into a hospital for wounded Indian soldiers. A wealth of photographs and some film footage document the story of this most famous military hospital in Britain.

After the war it was decided to turn this remote and windswept place on the Downs, 150 metres above sea level, where the cremations took place, into a site of remembrance. The young Indian architecture student E. C. Henriques was commissioned to design the monument, an 8.5-metre-tall, columned and domed temple in the Mughal style, made from white Sicilian marble, sitting on large grey stone terraces. On the plinth is an inscription in English, Hindi, Punjabi and Urdu, commemorating the soldiers. The Chattri was unveiled on 1 February, 1921.

The monument is all the more moving because it can only be reached on foot via a path off a bridleway between the A 27 bypass and the Clayton Windmills. You have to make an effort to find it, and the physical strain of reaching it adds to its poignancy. An annual remembrance ceremony takes place here in the second week of June.

Address Standean Lane, Patcham, BN1 8ZB, www.chattri.org | **Getting there By car:**
As you enter Brighton on the A 23, take the A 27 towards Lewes. At the second small
roundabout take the north exit into Braypool Lane and immediately turn right. Park on the
brow of the hill and walk to the Chattri by following the signposted footpath. **By bus:** any
bus to Patcham Old Village, then a 2 kilometres walk. | **Hours** Always accessible | **Tip** The
south gate of the Royal Pavilion also commemorates the Indian War Hospital (although
not the soldiers who died here). Known as the India Gate, it was given to Brighton by the
'princes and people of India' as a gesture of thanks for the care provided by the town's Indian
hospitals. It, too, was unveiled in 1921, by the Maharajah of Patiala.

18__ Clock Tower

Features an erratic golden time ball

In 1887, Victoria had been queen for 50 years. All around the country memorials were being commissioned to commemorate the golden jubilee, and clock towers were a particularly popular choice. Brighton decided to have one, too, and placed it on the north-west corner of the old fishing village, where West and North Street meet.

By the 1880s, this part of Brighton had changed considerably. The northward continuation of West Street was constructed in 1845 to link the station with the old part of town, and was named Queen's Road in honour of the sovereign. What better place to put a new shiny clock tower than at the junction of the old and the new?

The 23-metre-tall tower was designed by John Johnson and built in 1888, at a cost of £2,000. Its design is ornate and multi-coloured, comprising a variety of building materials, with a mishmash of classical and baroque elements. Four female figures sit around the tower on a granite plinth. Portraits of Queen Victoria, Prince Consort Albert, Edward, the Prince of Wales, and his wife, Alexandra, are on the four sides. Small ships protrude from pediments, giving directions to Hove, the sea, Kemptown and the railway station.

The crowning glory of the clock tower is a gilt-copper time ball, designed by Magnus Volks. It was supposed to move up and down a five-metre mast every full hour. The hydraulic mechanism was controlled by the Greenwich Observatory, but has hardly ever worked well or accurately. Don't expect to be able to set your watch by it, but it is fun watching out for golden ball movements.

By the mid-20th century, this landmark was considered worthless Victorian kitsch and only narrowly escaped demolition. Now it sits somewhat awkwardly surrounded by traffic, still underappreciated. It was restored in 2001–02 and looks particularly nice at Christmas time when decorated with hundreds of light chains in the shape of a canopy.

Address North Street/West Street/Queen's Road junction, nearest postcode BN1 1ZA | **Getting there** 5-minute walk from Brighton Railway Station; many buses to Clock Tower | **Tip** For the best view of the upper areas of the Clock Tower go into Waterstones bookshop at 71–74 North Street. The elegant five-storey building, built for Burton's tailors in 1928, with giant pilasters and deep cornices decorating the exterior, has cafés on the upper floors with windows offering direct views of the tower.

19 __ Devil's Dyke

Breathtaking highs and lows

Just five miles north of Brighton is a site of natural beauty that stunned the Romantic painter John Constable (see ch. 42) so much in the 1820s that he decided it was too grand to draw, as he couldn't possibly add anything to it. The place is Devil's Dyke, a V-shaped valley with hills rising more than 250 metres to either side.

The name derives from folklore: variants of a story circulate, in which the devil himself dug out the escarpment to flood the churches in the surrounding villages with seawater. He was interrupted in his vicious work, either by an old woman or because he injured his foot on a large rock. He left in a rage before finishing, and flung the rock towards the sea. It landed in Hove Park and is known as the Goldstone (see ch. 38) – and therein lies another story!

The dyke was actually formed over thousands of years through erosion and is the longest, deepest and widest dry valley in the UK. No surprise then that it became a major tourist attraction in the 19th century. Between 1887 and 1937 a single-track railway line ran between Hove and Devil's Dyke, and between 1894 and 1909 one of the UK's first cable-cars spanned the valley at a height of 70 metres, and a steep funicular took you from Poynings village to the top of the hillfort. Remains of these structures can still be seen.

The Devil's Dyke site is now cared for by The National Trust, and is also part of the South Downs National Park, with the South Downs Way running through it, so expect hikers and ramblers. Large signs illustrate walks and bike routes to suit everyone through the valley and beyond. Make sure to take in the views on both sides of the road: to the east is the dyke valley itself, whose free-roaming cattle help create the amazing carpet of flowers that appears in summer, while to the west you can enjoy perhaps the best panoramic view of the Sussex Weald. The sea shimmers on the southern horizon.

Address Dyke Road, +44 (0)1273 857712, www.nationaltrust.org.uk/devils-dyke, devilsdyke@nationaltrust.org.uk | **Getting there** Bus 77 to Devil's Dyke (open top in the summer); Devil's Dyke car park is approximately 3.5 kilometres north of the A 27, and just off the A 281 (signposted 'Devil's Dyke'); Satnav BN1 8YJ | **Tip** Don't dismiss the large Devil's Dyke Pub at the top of the hill. It may not look very rustic from the outside but manages to create a cosy atmosphere and serves decent food and drink. In fine weather and on Sundays/bank holidays booking is essential.

20 The Dome Foyer
Polychromatic oriental dreams

The Dome and Corn Exchange were built between 1803 and 1808 as the new stables and riding school for the Prince of Wales (later George IV). The imposing Dome provided rather lavish accommodation for the royal horses and was at the time the second-largest domed structure in the country after St Paul's Cathedral in London. The buildings, originally designed by William Porden, have gone through many changes, but retain their exotic features and grand proportions.

The Pavilion Estate was sold by Queen Victoria in 1850 and has since been in municipal ownership. The interiors of the Dome were remodelled in a highly ornamental style by Philip Lockwood in 1867, shortly after the addition of the museum and art gallery to the north (see ch. 29 and 51). More major structural changes came in 1901–02, when borough surveyor Francis J. May extended the museum, added a public library and constructed new entrances in Church Street. Although the Dome concert hall now sports a 1930s' Art Deco scheme, the magnificent glazed tiles and columns in the foyer and staircases are stunning survivors of this earlier scheme.

The polychromatic tiles and the matching mosaic floors have a Moorish flavour to them and were most probably chosen as a nod to the oriental features of the Royal Pavilion and stables. Interlocking turquoise and green tiles unite the decorative scheme and can be seen throughout the foyer and the northern corridors of the museum. The tiles were designed by architect G. Harold Elphick and made by Craven Dunhill & Co of Jackfield, Shropshire. Founded in 1872, the company is still in existence and helped with restoration work here in 2002.

The beauty of the tiles soon made the papers. On 1 November, 1902, *The Brighton Herald* noted that 'the finest work in this faience is in the corridor leading to the Dome. Here the art of the ceramic worker is revealed to a degree almost magnificent'.

Concert Hall Circle Left ↗

Address Church Street, BN1 1UE, +44 (0)1273 709709, brightondome.org | Getting
there 10-minute walk from Brighton Railway Station; many buses to North Street or Old
Steine | Hours Accessibility varies depending on events at the Dome. If closed, peer through
the iron gates of the north entrances to get a glimpse of the tiles, or look for some in the
museum. | Tip Walk 3 minutes north along Jubilee Street (memorialised in 2013 by local
musician Nick Cave in a song of the same title) and you see Jubilee Library, a design award-
winning public library, built in 2005.

21 Dovecote, Patcham
Room for 550 high-status doves

Patcham is a residential area on the northern outskirts of Brighton, bordering the A27 bypass. Most people arriving by car via the London Road whizz past it, but it is worth a visit, as it boasts many old and beautiful buildings and structures. Now swallowed up by Brighton's sprawl, it was once an independent village, covering a large area north of Preston.

In the 11th-century Domesday Book, a kind of inventory of the country compiled by the Norman conquerors, it is listed as having a population of up to 1,750. This made it one of the largest settlements in the county – certainly larger than Brighton, and a lot leafier – but by the early 19th century, when Brighton was in its heyday, its population had dwindled to no more than 500.

Its ancient history is the reason for the many architectural gems you find here, from grand houses and old farm buildings to exquisite flint and half-timbered cottages. These sit side by side with modern developments and houses, all of them thankfully low structures, unlike the many 1960s' high-rises that line London Road in nearby Preston and Withdean.

A particularly delightful structure is the dovecote of the old Patcham Court Farm. The farm was recorded in the Domesday Book and covered more than 700 acres. It has long ceased to be a farm, but several of its 17th-century buildings survive, including the farmhouse itself and the weather-boarded tithe barn, the longest in Sussex, measuring 228 metres. Both have been converted into private dwellings. In the back garden of the farmhouse is the Grade II-listed circular dovecote. It was built of brick and local flint in the early 17th century or earlier, and has survived largely intact, with 550 nesting boxes. It is a fine example of this type of high-status building, often associated with manor houses. Another example can be seen in the garden of Hangleton Manor (see ch. 39).

Address Vale Avenue/Church Hill, BN1 8YF | **Getting there** 20-minute walk from Preston Park Station; bus 5 to Patcham Old Village; some parking nearby | **Hours** Not open to the public. The dovecote is on private land but is visible from Church Hill. | **Tip** Further down on the other side of London Road is a 1930s' development called the Brangwyn Estate, after the Ditchling-based artist and designer Frank Brangwyn. Two chunky, red-brick posts with Art Deco lamps designed by him stand at its entrance in Brangwyn Drive. The nearest bus stop is Ridgeside Avenue.

22 The Dragon Chandelier
An extraordinary flight of fancy

The Banqueting Room of the Royal Pavilion is a sparkling, heavily ornamented interior. The most flamboyant object in the room, and arguably in the entire building, is the 9-metre-long, one-ton central crystal chandelier. The design is fantastical, topped by a dragon with wings outstretched, under an illusionist ceiling painting of an exotic plantain tree. The dragon seems to be holding the heavy chandelier in its claws, but of course it doesn't bear the weight; it hides a strong cast iron construction, suspended from the tent-shaped roof.

Designed in or just after 1817 by Welsh artist Robert Jones, the dragon was carved from various types of wood, then silvered and eventually glazed with layers of translucent paint.

One can imagine that after several hours of excessive eating and drinking, guests would have felt dizzy and disoriented when they looked up at the ceiling. Some guests in the 1820s expressed their concern about the dragon letting go of the chandelier. It seems that Queen Caroline (wife of William IV) had similar concerns, as she replaced it with a lighter one in the 1830s. It was reinstated for Queen Victoria's visits to the Pavilion a few years later, and she eventually took it with her to Kensington Palace in the 1840s, although she returned it to the Pavilion in the 1860s, never having installed it. One wonders whether she found it a little too imposing, or whether it was simply too large for any of the rooms at the London palaces.

The chandelier certainly developed its own mythology. The Victorian historian J. G. Bishop repeatedly wrote that it was sent out in 1814 with Lord Macartney's embassy to China as a present to the emperor and, following the failure of the negotiations, was brought back to England. Bishop got both the dates of the Macartney Embassy (1792–94) and the creation of the chandelier wrong. Needless to say, it never travelled to China.

Address The Royal Pavilion, 4/5 Pavilion Buildings, BN1 1EE, +44 (0)1273 071273, brightonmuseums.org.uk/royalpavilion, info@rpmt.org.uk | Getting there 3-minute walk from the Old Steine; many buses to Old Steine | Hours Daily Oct–Mar 10am–5.15pm, Apr–Sep 9.30am–5.45pm | Tip If you are a fan of crime fiction, read Peter James's thriller Not Dead Yet, the eighth in the popular series featuring Detective Superintendent Roy Grace. The Dragon Chandelier plays a starring role in it.

23 Embassy Court
The best of British seaside Modernism

This magnificent 11-storey building on the corner of King's Road and Western Street resembles an ocean liner about to cross the Atlantic. Designed by the charismatic architect Wells Coates in 1935, it is one of the sleekest and most elegant examples of British Modernist architecture and design. But it wasn't always appreciated and fell into disrepair in the later 20th century, when tastes had changed and Modernism had become a negative term for many.

Built for Maddox Properties, it stands on the site of a demolished two-storey villa and a miniature golf course. The investors clearly understood the value of this plot of land, but the building of such a radically modern and tall building was controversial. Then and now, it forms a stark contrast to its neighbouring Regency buildings. This is particularly apparent on the south front, where the Regency town houses next door rise to just half its height.

Coates, a Canadian, was influenced by many cultures and movements. The rounded south-east corner, subtle recessed upper floors and the attention to minimalist detail perhaps reflect his upbringing in Japan. He was also clearly aware of the work of European architects such as Berthold Lubetkin, Erich Mendelsohn, Marcel Breuer and Le Corbusier, whom he met on several occasions. The building materials are typical of inter-war Modernism: reinforced concrete, combined with steel used for window and door frames. The 72 flats in Embassy Court were designed for rich people: in the early years the annual rent could be as much as the price of a small house in the area.

By the 1970s, the building was rusty, the white render had faded into grey. Many of the flats lay empty and the building became a symbol of seaside seediness and decay. Between 2004 and 2006 it was completely renovated and now looks ultra-chic again, but it still divides opinion.

Address Kings Road, BN1 2PY, www.embassycourt.org.uk | Getting there 20-minute walk from Brighton Railway Station; many buses to Norfolk Square | Hours Not open to the public, but the residents of Embassy Court occasionally give guided tours of the building, which are advertised on the website | Tip At the other end of Brighton, overlooking the Marina (see ch. 52), is Marine Gate, another iconic but less well-known example of a Modernist block of flats. Built in 1939 by Wimperis, Simpson & Guthrie, its style is streamlined, like Embassy Court, with strong emphasis on horizontal lines and some nautically inspired features.

24_ Emmaus, Portslade

Fighting homelessness with kindness and creativity

Emmaus is an international charity that originated in France in the 1940s and now has 29 communities across the UK. It tackles homelessness and poverty by engaging those in need in setting up workshops, looking after cafés and shops, and essentially running small businesses in the Emmaus communities. Companions, as they are called, are given a stable home, sign off all state benefits and instead work in the community for 40 hours a week or as much as they can. The aim is for the community to become self-sufficient and the companion to regain confidence and pride in their work.

The Brighton community, located in the Old Portslade Village on the site of a Norman manor house and its 19th-century replacement, is a particularly special Emmaus branch. Don't expect a charity shop though. This is a social hub, where you can easily spend half a day browsing, shopping, eating, looking at historic monuments, or taking part in one of the many events they put on. It is the largest of the Emmaus branches in the UK, with 48 companions, 11 staff and 8 trustees, and has been playing a huge role in Portslade and the larger Brighton community since its beginnings here in 1997.

Among the things you can do here is find good-quality secondhand furniture at very reasonable prices (many young Brightonians have kitted out their first home with Emmaus furniture), have a classic English breakfast in the Revive café, stock up on plants and seedlings for your garden (grown on site and displayed outside and in a pretty greenhouse extension), donate your own unwanted things, or enjoy the community garden and let the children run wild in the play areas. A large general Secondhand Superstore has recently had a complete revamp and now features the classy Emporium, where you find stylish vintage clothes, bric-a-brac and furniture. The place oozes positivity, humanity and solidarity.

Address Drove Road, BN41 2PA, +44 (0)1273 426480, www.emmaus.org.uk/brighton_hove, contact@emmausbrighton.co.uk | **Getting there** Best reached by car (some free parking available), or bus 1, 1A to St Nicolas Church, Portslade | **Hours** Mon–Sat 9.30am–5pm, café closed Mon | **Tip** The ancient Church of St Nicolas abuts the Emmaus site and can be seen through the windows of the Superstore. In front of it are the ruins of the Norman manor house, and nearby is a similar-looking folly, created from the stones of the Victorian manor.

25 English's of Brighton

A seemingly timeless oyster bar

Brighton is teeming with new, exciting and experimental restaurants, but if you want to be transported back in time, treat yourself to a meal at English's at the heart of the Lanes, a stone's throw from the Royal Pavilion. Comprising three 18th-century former fishermen's cottages, it is the oldest restaurant in Brighton and has become one of the most famous seafood restaurants in England. Its signature dishes are Dover sole, lobster, and of course oysters, sourced from the shallow creeks leading from the River Blackwater to the west of Mersey Island in Essex, and from the Lindisfarne Oyster Farm in the north of England. Wherever possible, other seafood is sourced locally.

English's started as 'Brazier's Fishmongers' over 150 years ago, and some brass-work and marble of its earliest incarnation can still be seen on the outside of the building. In the early 20th century, Mr English married one of the Brazier daughters and established an oyster bar. In 1945, immediately after the end of World War II, the father of the current owner Simon Leigh-Jones bought the establishment and the two cottages on either side, so for more than 70 years English's has been with the same family.

The restaurant has had an extremely illustrious stream of guests, including none other than Charlie Chaplin, among other mid-20th-century film and theatre stars. More recently Judy Dench, Ian McKellen and Richard E. Grant have enjoyed dining here. Check the walls for autographs and pictures left by glamourous guests. The decoration of the ground floor rooms has a touch of 1920s' Paris about it, while the larger rooms on the upper floor were painted by local art students Catarna Perestrello and Mark Davies in 1996. The charming murals show Edwardian dinner scenes and images inspired by Oscar Wilde's play *The Importance of Being Earnest*. Can you spot Oscar Wilde himself among them?

Address 29–31 East Street, BN1 1HL, +44 (0)1273 327980, www.englishs.co.uk | **Getting there** 15-minute walk from Brighton Railway Station, 3-minute walk from the Royal Pavilion; many buses to Old Steine | **Hours** Daily noon–10pm | **Tip** From here you can start exploring the street pattern that constituted the old fishing town. 'Dipper' Martha Gunn (see ch. 53) lived at 36 East Street. East Street formed the eastern boundary of medieval Brighton and leads down to the seafront. Go down smaller lanes and alleyways such as Market Street or Little East Street to find out more about Brighton's historic layout.

26 Extra-Mural Cemetery

Who needs Père Lachaise?

By the mid-19th century, the rapidly expanding Brighton and Hove needed a separate town just for its dead. Plans were made for a landscaped 13-acre site on the outskirts of town: the Extra-Mural Cemetery, which first opened in 1851. By 1853, burials were no longer allowed in the immediate vicinity of churches in the town, so in 1857 the site was enlarged by a further 8 acres, and a further 20-acre cemetery was added to the south (now the Brighton Borough Cemetery).

The initial cemetery was laid out in Gothic style by famous Brighton architect Amon Henry Wilds (see ch. 27, 48, 62, 81 and 91). Approached via a long straight path from the traffic-heavy Lewes Road, visitors soon find themselves in a dreamlike world of sweeping avenues, ancient elm trees, crumbling High Victorian tombstones in the shapes of crosses, pinnacles and Egyptian obelisks. Angels and saints make melancholy gestures, tombs are overgrown with ivy. There is an eerie stillness to the place. A marvellous Gothic flint chapel and a mausoleum interrupt the tightly packed graves and tombs lining the north side of the cemetery, and the place is a haven for anyone with an interest in photographing the gloomy beauty of decay and the iconography of the Victorian 'cult of death'. In as early as 1864, guidebooks to the cemetery were published, suggesting recreational strolls, praising both the natural and cultivated beauty of it.

Many famous 19th-century Brightonians are buried here. and their tombstones often tell their story. The towering 1861 John Collingwood tomb resembles a Gothic tabernacle; the most imposing, that of railway engineer John Rastrick (see ch. 13 and 48) is a huge granite tomb in the shape of a railway turntable. The cemetery has helpful signage for circular 'tomb and nature walks', and even a designated picnic site near the entrance, should you need sustenance before losing yourself in the land of the dead.

Address Lewes Road, BN2 3QB | Getting there 15-minute walk from London Road Railway Station; many buses to Lewes Road Bus Garage | Tip If you are in the mood for even more Gothic gloom, visit the nearby chapels at Woodvale Crematorium, built in 1856 and refurbished in 2013.

27 Fabrica

Contemporary art in a Regency church

Brighton has a thriving visual and performing arts scene, a renowned art college and a fabulous municipal art gallery, so it is only right that it should have a place like Fabrica, where young and established artists are nurtured, supported and given a spacious arena to show their work. Since 1996 it has been the hub for cutting-edge contemporary installation art, most of it created specifically for this site.

The site is very special indeed: Fabrica occupies Holy Trinity Church in Ship Street in the Lanes, a deconsecrated church dating from 1817, built by architect Amon Wilds (father of Amon Henry Wilds) for the greatest developer and landowner of the town, Thomas Read Kemp (see ch. 43 and 47). It was originally independent and Nonconformist, according to Kemp's wishes, but later became an Anglican chapel. It went through several redevelopments and uses, then closed in 1985. Several ideas were being floated about what to do with the building.

Eventually, the Brighton artists' collective Red Herring Studios took over the building and turned it into an exciting place for contemporary visual art installations, under the early formative guidance of founding member Matthew Miller and with support from South East Arts, Brighton Borough Council and other bodies. The name was chosen because it expresses making, creating and producing things and sounds similar in several European languages, expressing creativity and invention.

The first exhibition was staged in 1996 and Fabrica has since played a major role in the annual Brighton Festival. Over the years it has hosted some impressive displays of works by new and well-known artists, including the mesmerising light installation 77 Million Paintings by musician and producer Brian Eno in 2010, and two works by Anish Kapoor, one of them in collaboration with novelist Salman Rushdie, for the 2009 Brighton Festival.

Address 40 Duke Street, BN1 1AG, +44 (0)1273 778646, www.fabrica.org.uk, office@fabrica.org.uk | **Getting there** 10-minute walk from Brighton Railway Station; many buses to North Street | **Hours** Open for events only. Check website for details. | **Tip** Apart from site-specific exhibitions, Fabrica runs a programme of events, including talks, workshops and film screenings, and invites volunteers to become involved in the running of the gallery. A free reference library is available to artists and researchers.

28__Falmer House

Abstract art and gleaming flint for lunch

Falmer House was the first of the unflinchingly modern campus buildings, designed by Sir Basil Spence for Sussex University in the early 1960s, to be finished. The proud gateway to the University, lauded for its clean lines and underlying ideas of transparency, confidence and accessibility, stood for a new era in education, style and fashion. Sussex was the ultimate hip and modern university, and Falmer House was the designated seat of the Students' Union. Through its large glass and steel windows, students could watch over the internal moated courtyard and see who was coming and going – and they still do. It is one of very few 20th-century educational buildings that has been given the Grade I Listed Building status, and is a much-admired, but also often criticised, masterpiece of mid-20th-century architecture.

As with all his campus buildings, Spence emphasised the subtle interaction of material, light and colour (see ch. 76). Sunlight bounces off the knapped flint wall in the main staircase and floods Mandela Hall, a double-height area with a mezzanine, approached from the first floor. Now a multi-functional room, it once housed the dining hall. In keeping with the Modernist look, ornament and decoration are kept to an absolute minimum. But a surprise awaits in Mandela Hall: high on its north wall hangs *Day's Rest, Day's Work*, a spectacular seven-metre-long abstract painting of overlapping, intertwining shapes and lines in warm and sumptuous colours. It was created in 1962 for this site by Ivon Hitchens, who in the 1920s and 1930s had been working with other renowned Modernist artists such as Barbara Hepworth, Henry Moore and Ben Nicholson. His use of colour was inspired by French Post-Impressionists. Based in West Sussex for many years, he became known for his abstract landscapes, some of which are in museums in Sussex, but nowhere can you see one on such a scale, in its original location.

Address University of Sussex, Falmer, BN1 9QF | Getting there 5-minute walk from Falmer Railway Station; bus 5b, 23, 25, 25X, 28, 29, 29B, 29X, 50 to Falmer Station | Hours Generally open during the day on weekdays. Visitors are welcome but events may be going on in the building, restricting access. | Tip If you have had enough of mid-20th-century Modernism, head south, cross the bypass and the railway bridge and visit the ancient Falmer Village. Originally a Saxon Downland village, it has a lovely pond, church and a 13th-century thatched barn.

29 Fashion & Style Gallery
Sartorial glamour and grit

Brighton Museum is a typical example of Victorian municipal museum culture (see ch. 51), but it has moved with the times, and since its 19th-century beginnings developed new collections that illustrate more recent and contemporary culture, often with direct links to Brighton's social and cultural history.

On the upper floor you will find a large gallery dedicated to the museum's costume collection, which began in 1897 with the donation of a blue silk umbrella. Since then it has grown to a collection of significant national importance, containing more than 10,000 items. The oldest pieces date from the 16th century, and, given the impact of George IV on the city, there are fine examples of Regency costume, including George's enormous breeches, and a dress worn by one of the 'herb-strewer' women, who scattered flowers at his coronation in 1821.

But what is truly remarkable about this collection is its sheer breadth and variety. It encompasses dress from European and North American culture, and inspired by geographically distant cultures. There are stunning examples of national and international fashion by famous designers such as Norman Hartnell, Mary Quant and Alexander McQueen. A highlight are several women's dresses from six generations of the West-Sussex Messel family. These fine costumes sit side by side with the Renegade collection, comprising complete outfits from the last 60 years, once worn by Brightonians who rejected mainstream fashion and used dress as a form of rebellion or a symbol of belonging to a counter-culture group, such as Punks, Hippies, Goths or Skaters. The latest addition to the collection is a group of some 20 'queer looks' outfits and oral histories, which reflect the last 50 years of LGBTQ+ history in Brighton. Because of the size of the collection, displays alternate in the gallery, but you will always see a combination of glamour and grit.

Address Brighton Museum & Art Gallery, Royal Pavilion Gardens, BN1 1EE, +44 (0)1273 071273, brightonmuseums.org.uk/brighton/exhibitions-displays/fashion-and-style, info@rpmt.org.uk | Getting there 15-minute walk from Brighton Railway Station; many buses to Old Steine or North Street | Hours Tue–Sun 10am–5pm, closed Mon (except bank holidays), 24 Dec (from 2.30pm) and 25 & 26 Dec | Tip There are more examples of fashion, dress and textiles dotted elsewhere around the museum. Look for colourful examples in the World Stories gallery on the ground floor, or see fancy dress and carnival costumes in the Performance gallery on the upper floor.

30_Fingermaze
A labyrinth for the mind

Hove Park is an enormous green lung and social space in the city, covering a crescent-shaped area of almost 40 acres from the Old Shoreham Road in the south to Woodland Drive in the north. It has a large children's playground, tennis and basketball courts, football fields, cafés and, of course, beautiful trees and greenery.

It also has a few more unusual attractions (see ch. 38). One of these is the *Fingermaze*, a subtle piece of public sculpture on the park's eastern edge that invites you to walk, reflect and calm your thoughts. Designed in 2004 by land artist Chris Drury, who also created the *Heart of Reeds* sculpture for Lewes railway land (see ch. 104), *Fingermaze* was originally conceived as a temporary piece drawn into the grass at Stanmer Park before being recreated in this more permanent form in 2006.

The work, carved into a gentle slope, is a linear pattern resembling a giant human fingerprint. It is made from randomly shaped pieces of York flagstone set into the ground, held together by lime mortar. The whiteness of the stone reminds one of the ancient chalk carvings found on Sussex and Kent hills. Lime mortar was used as its production uses considerably less energy than making cement. Strictly speaking it is not a maze but a labyrinth, based on ancient patterns of one singular meandering path leading to a centre point. It invites us to just wander along the path without being distracted by decisions about which turn to take.

Finding the *Fingermaze* is part of its experience. Sunk into the ground, it is not immediately visible, and only becomes a three-dimensional piece of sculpture once entered. As was intended, it has weathered over time, its edges blurred and its colours have darkened. It is slowly becoming assimilated into the landscape of Hove Park, until perhaps only faint outlines will be visible, like the traces of ancient structures and settlements seen from the air.

Address Hove Park, nearest postcode BN3 7BF, www.brighton-hove.gov.uk | Getting there 10-minute walk from Hove Railway Station; bus 21E, 56, 59A, 59E to Hove Park; time-limited free parking along Goldstone Crescent | Hours Always accessible | Tip You may have come to Hove Park by train, but if you want to ride a miniature version of a functioning steam train, head to the north-western edge of the park, where you will find the 610-metre-long Hove Park Railway, run by a team of steam engine enthusiasts (www.hoveparkrailway.co.uk).

31__Flint Grotto
A magical rocky garden by the sea

In the middle of the beach halfway between Brighton Pier and the Marina is a small fenced area with sculptural formations made from beach pebbles and shells. Locals have been following the slow formation of this strange little rock garden since the turn of the millennium.

For centuries, the old fishing village of Brighton consisted of an intricate network of low-rise, flint, fishermen's cottages, huddled together in what is now the Lanes area. There is now little left of the old fishing industry that once dominated the seafront, but a few individual fishermen still carry on. In the past they would leave their fishing gear in wooden stores on the beach, but these have all been demolished. However, the council has allocated small plots of land where they can keep their boats, lobster pots, nets and other equipment.

Rory McCormack has been fishing on the beach for decades, since he was a teenager, and keeps everything fishing-related he can't fit into his small flat on one of these plots. Also, over the years he has been creating a magical garden here, using almost exclusively what he finds under his feet on the beach. It all began when he made himself a workbench out of flint and decorated with shells he had been collecting for years. Statues resembling ancient gods and goddesses soon followed, sturdy figures rightly likened to outsider art or Arte Povera. They are raw, unconventional, and strangely moving, standing silently, battered by wind, sun and water, among small vegetable patches, paths and shelters that look as if the sea itself has grown them.

Although McCormack's creation seems entirely innocent, and is surrounded by a seven-foot fence, the council has decreed it a health-and-safety risk. Petitions are regularly launched to protect the grotto – a wonderful example of someone living and working closely with the sea and taking inspiration from it.

Address On the beach by Madeira Drive, nearest postcode BN2 1AE | **Getting there** 30-minute walk from Brighton Railway Station, or a leisurely 10-minute walk east from Brighton Pier; bus 12, 12A, 14, 27 to Bedford Street South | **Tip** To reach the grotto you need to cross rail tracks where the beach meets Madeira Drive. These belong to the narrow-gauge Volks Electric Railway, created by clockmaker Magnus Volks in 1883. It operated from opposite the Aquarium to the Chain Pier, taking Brighton visitors along the beach. After major restoration it is now running again during the summer months (volkselectricrailway.co.uk).

32 Fly Stables
Garages for Regency mini-cabs

In a little-known side street near Churchill Square, an unassuming, symmetrical assembly of low structures with haylofts and projecting garages of sorts was in 2012 identified as possibly the only surviving examples of early 19th-century 'fly' stables.

A fly was a small, light, low carriage, ideal for short distances. The Regency equivalent to the mini-cab, they were particularly popular in Brighton, and might have originated here. Unlike a normal coach or hansom cab, they were most commonly pulled by manpower (or boypower). These 'man-flys' were likely the best mode of transport in Brighton's old town centre where the thoroughfares were far narrower and windier than they are today. They were probably used especially after visits to vapour baths. A 'fly-by-night' could get you home late at night, preferably unnoticed. Once the town spread out, horse-drawn flys or hansom cabs were quicker and better suited for travelling greater distances.

An 1818 guidebook instructs: 'The local conveyances in Brighton are innumerable. A nouvelle kind of four-wheel vehicles, drawn by a man and an assistant are very accommodating to visitors and the inhabitants. They are denominated flys, a name given by a gentleman at the Pavilion on their first introduction in 1816.' This date is later corrected by historian John Erredge, who tells us the vehicle was invented in 1809: 'During the erection of the Royal Stables, in Church Street, in 1809, a carpenter . . . accidentally fell and injured himself . . . [N]ot being able to resume the heavy work of his trade, he constructed a machine of similar make to the sedan chair, and placed it upon four wheels. It was drawn by hand, in the same manner as Bath chairs, while an assistant, when the person was heavy, pushed behind.'

The Stone Street fly stables were saved from demolition and are now on the National Heritage List.

Address 13A and 14 Stone Street, Brighton, BN1 2HB | Getting there 15-minute walk from Brighton Railway Station; many buses to Churchill Square, then 5-minute walk | Hours Private property and not open to the public | Tip It is worth spending some time in the area, as some handsome Regency-period buildings survive nearby, despite the encroachment of the shopping areas. Particularly nice are the cast-iron balconies of the south side of Russell Square.

33 Foredown Tower

From dangerous viruses to distant views

If you are not afraid of heights and have perhaps enjoyed a ride on the British Airways i360 (see ch. 14) but want to see more of Sussex Downs instead of an urban landscape from an elevated position, then this tower is the place to head for. Foredown Tower sits high on the north-western edge of Brighton and offers amazing views over the surrounding countryside. What's more, it comes with a very special device that makes the viewing experience even more exciting.

The square, red-brick tower was built in 1909 as a water tower for the Victorian Foredown Isolation Hospital. Since the 1880s, the hospital had treated patients with infectious diseases such as smallpox, diphtheria and tuberculosis, which explains the tower's remote location. It must have been a bleak place for both patients and staff up there on the Downs. Unsurprisingly, the death rate at the hospital was high, and the tower was occasionally used as a mortuary. The hospital closed in in the early 1970s and was briefly used as a home for disabled children, before it was closed and the buildings became derelict.

The hospital building was demolished, but thankfully the tower was saved and underwent a complete transformation in 1991 into a centre for astronomical studies. The largest operational camera obscura in the South East was installed in the tower, and it received its distinctive conical top.

It has been run by several organisations since then. At the moment it is operated and maintained by Portslade Adult Learning, which regularly opens the Learning and Visitor Centre to the public. You can climb the tower and either enjoy panoramic views over Sussex, or observe the sun and sky through the camera obscura, but the latter is weather dependent. There is a small café and a peaceful garden. Unfortunately, there is wheelchair access to ground floor only, as there is no lift in the tower.

Address Foredown Road, BN41 2EW, +44 (0)1273 415625, www.brighton-hove.gov.uk |
Getting there 30-minute walk from Portslade Railway Station; bus 6 or 95A to Foredown
Road, walk up the hill, cross Fox Way and follow signs | Hours Call to check opening and
demonstration time | Tip Foredown Tower runs a variety of courses for adults focussing
on or starting at the tower, for example painting in watercolour. For details, download a
brochure from the Portslade website: www.portslade.org.

34__Freemasons Tavern
A Klimt-like facelift for an old inn

Brighton and Hove are best known for their white and cream Georgian Terraces (see ch. 47), the oriental fantasies found on the Royal Pavilion Estate, and the occasional Modernist masterpiece, such as Embassy Court (see ch. 23). But every now and again you spot something unique. The Freemasons Tavern is one of these buildings.

From the outside it looks like a slice of the best Viennese Art Deco style transplanted into the Georgian Brunswick Estate, an area on the border of Brighton and Hove that was developed from 1825 by the architect Charles Busby for the increasing number of wealthy visitors to the town. So why is there a shimmering blue-and-gold façade gracing the building?

The Freemasons Tavern occupies the corner block of Western Road and Brunswick Street West. It probably dates from the early 1850s and was most likely purpose-built as an inn, as a list of early landlords confirms. Its major makeover occurred in 1928, when the local Kemp Town Brewery took it over and decided on a complete refit, relabelling it a restaurant. They hired prolific architect John Leopold Denman, who could turn his hand to pretty much anything: mansions, churches, cemeteries, hotels and other public buildings. At the time of this commission, Denman was the head of the Department of Architecture of the Brighton School of Art, and Brighton is peppered with his buildings, most of which were created during the high demand for civic buildings in the 1930s.

Here he opted for an unusual amount of joyful glamour and mystery: the north frontage of the tavern is covered in shimmering mosaics and masonic symbols, and a double-height bronze-and-glass screen forms the entrance. Some Art Deco friezes and ornaments survive on the inside. It is now a pub famous for its wild late-night music events. Daytimes are calmer, and decent food and drink is available.

Address 38–39 Western Road, BN3 1AF, +44(0)1273 732043, www.freemasons.pub, hello@freemasons.pub | **Getting there** 20-minute walk from Brighton Railway Station; bus 1, 1A, 2, 5, 5A, 5B to Brunswick Place | **Hours** Fri & Sat noon–2.30am, Sun–Thu noon–late | **Tip** A 5-minute walk west along Western Road takes you to the northern end of Palmeira Square. Gwydr Gentlemen's Hairdressers, on the corner of Holland Road and Church Road, is an old-fashioned barber in the basement of Gwydr Mansions. Established in 1896, it has retained many early features, including fittings from 1936.

35 — French Protestant Church

Standing dignified among giants

In the second half of the 19th century, Brighton was a thriving sea-side resort and holiday destination. It was then that the large hotels on King's Road were built; the Grand in 1862, followed by the even larger Metropole in 1890. The Metropole Hotel is a sight to behold, taking up an entire street block, with sprawling extensions to the north. Follow the narrow Queensbury Mews next to the hotel and there is a – literally – little surprise in store. Among the soaring Victorian and 20th-century high-rises sits a small red brick church with a pitched roof and Gothic windows with quatrefoil tracery.

This charming building is the French Protestant Church of Brighton (L'Eglise Française Réformée), built in 1887 to designs by J. G. Gibbins, as a place of worship for the French Protestant community in the area. As this coincided with Queen Victoria's Golden Jubilee (see ch. 18), a time capsule containing objects associated with the event was inserted into the foundation stone. The church also served the large number of visitors from France, which may explain its location so close to the seafront. It predated the only other French Protestant church in the country, in London's Soho Square.

In the 16th century, many Protestants facing Catholic persecution on the continent fled to England. The French Protestant Church of London was founded in 1550 and similar communities were emerging in Brighton. Under the Catholic rule of Queen Mary I they faced further threats here (see ch. 105) and often met in secret in private houses. In 1887, the French congregation and Brighton's religious community raised money for the building of this permanent place of worship. The church was consecrated in 1888 and served the French community until its closure in 2008. It is now a private house but at least it dodged demolition.

Address Queensbury Mews, BN1 2FE | **Getting there** 20-minute walk from Brighton Railway Station; many buses to Churchill Square | **Hours** Not open to the public | **Tip** Speaking of small buildings among structures of Manhattan-style dimensions, just opposite the church is The Queensbury Arms pub, allegedly the smallest pub in Brighton and formerly known as 'The Hole in the Wall'. Its interior is plush and cosy, as you would expect from a traditional English pub.

36 Friends Meeting House

An oasis of calm and openness

The history of Brighton's Quakers dates back as far as 1655 when young Nicholas Beard of Rottingdean (see ch. 45, 78 and 87) began preaching Quaker values and beliefs in Sussex. For this he was persecuted and imprisoned in Lewes. Undeterred, in 1659 he bought grounds for a Quaker burial site in Rottingdean. Around the same time, the first Quaker meetings were held in private houses in Brighton, and Beard and others began preaching in local churches, or 'steeple houses'.

By 1700, the Quaker community had increased and become more organised, despite continued persecution. The first meeting house for worship was created in a converted malt house in North Street. A narrow stretch of land to the north was also appropriated and became known as Quakers' Croft, with a small burial ground at its far end. This is roughly the area by the double row of large trees on the western edge of the Royal Pavilion Gardens.

By the time the disreputable Prince of Wales arrived in Brighton in the 1780s, the Quaker community counted around 45 members. The prince was eager to expand his estate and in 1806 bought Quakers' Croft to incorporate it into his gardens and build stables for his illegal wife, Maria Fitzherbert.

The new and more solid meeting house in Ship Street was built in 1805, but was much altered in 1850 and in 1876, when a new north wing was added. The surrounding burial ground is no longer in use, but has become a peaceful oasis in the hustle and bustle of the Lanes area. The meeting house has a welcoming feel and many public events take place in the main hall, which has retained its basic layout.

Although this has been the main seat of Brighton Quakers now for over 200 years, the Quakers were recently called back to the original site: in 2017, during major building work at the Corn Exchange and Dome (see ch. 20), more than a dozen graves with human remains were excavated in what used to be Quakers' Croft.

Address Ship Street, BN1 1AF, +44 (0)1273 770258, www.brightonquakers.co.uk | Getting there 12-minute walk from Brighton Railway Station; many buses to Old Steine | Hours No specified opening times. See website for events. | Tip When leaving the meeting house gardens, turn left into Prince Albert Street and find Meeting House Lane, which forms the back and eastern boundary of the estate. The flint wall of this lane is not just a typical example of the use of simple, local materials, it is also allegedly haunted by a 'grey nun', who has been seen disappearing into a bricked-up doorway.

37 George and Victoria
Uncle and niece united in stone

Brighton is peppered with monuments to Queen Victoria, but relatively few acknowledge the impact King George IV had on the town. This might just be indicative of how the two were judged in respect of their morals and behaviour, or of what the council's motivations were for erecting their statues.

If the relationships between each monarch and Brighton were complex, so was their relationship with each other. It is quite amusing seeing them immortalised in two large statues in central Brighton, in close proximity to each other and to the Royal Pavilion. It looks a little bit like a stand-off or staring competition, albeit unintended. Both statues are public art of some merit, and the story they tell is very much one of Brighton's history.

George IV, who was Victoria's uncle, is represented in a replica of a sculpture commissioned by him from Sir Francis Chantrey, a leading portrait sculptor of his time. Chantrey also made the equestrian figure of George IV that is on one of the plinths in Trafalgar Square, London. A marble version of the sculpture is on the Grand Staircase outside the Waterloo Chamber in Windsor Castle. This copy was unveiled in 1828, not where you see it now, outside the North Gate of the Pavilion Estate (see ch. 71). Until 1922 it was in a central place on the Steine but was moved to make way for a World War I memorial (see ch. 86 Tip).

Victoria, who ascended the throne in 1837, was famously disapproving of both her disreputable uncle and Brighton, and quickly decided to disassociate herself with both, selling the entire Pavilion Estate in 1850. The town tried hard to please her, welcoming her with lavish ceremonies on her few visits, but to no avail. Even after she left, they kept erecting monuments to her, like this one by Carlo Nicoli, placed here in 1897 when the Victoria Gardens were opened, to commemorate the Queen's Diamond Jubilee.

Address Victoria Gardens, BN1 1WN | Getting there A few steps from the North Gate of the Royal Pavilion; many buses to Old Steine | Hours Always accessible | Tip For a good photo opportunity, wait until a disrespectful seagull lands on either monarch's head. Victoria Gardens is usually the site of much cultural activity during the Brighton Festival.

38 The Goldstone

The Devil's work, or Druidic stone circle?

The area around the southwest corner of Hove Park is known as Goldstone Bottom. For hundreds of years this shallow valley stretching northward from the Old Shoreham Road was farmland. One doesn't really expect much to have happened in such a rural area, but in the past this spot has been the site of much excitement concerning a huge rock.

The name was given to the area because a mysterious large rock, known as 'The Goldstone', lay for many years on the farmland. The rugged stone, a mixture of sandstone and flint conglomerate weighs a whopping 20 tons, stands nearly 3 metres high and is surrounded by a circle of smaller stones.

Many myths concerning its origins and meaning developed around the Goldstone and people visited in droves. One of the legends was that the Devil himself stubbed his foot on the stone while digging out Devil's Dyke (see ch. 19), an escarpment north of Brighton, in a vicious attempt to flood churches nearby. In a rage, he threw the stone towards the sea, and it landed on the corner of what is now Hove Park (see ch. 30). Some claimed to have seen the face of God in the texture of the stone, causing its name sometimes to be recorded as 'Godstone'. Others believed that the group of stones were part of a Druids' altar and therefore sacred.

In the 1830s, the swelling number of visitors flocking to the mystical stones was beginning to annoy the landowner and farmer, Mr William Marsh Rigden, as it was causing damage to his crops. He took matters into his own hands and buried the stones in a secret place. Given their size and weight one wonders how he managed to do this. They lay hidden until rediscovered by Hove Commissioner William Hollamby in 1900. He perhaps saw a marketing opportunity for the new public park being developed and installed them in their current position in the south-west corner of Hove Park in 1906, just after it opened.

Address Hove Park, Park View Road, BN3 7BF | Getting there 10-minute walk from Hove Railway Station; bus 21E, 56, 59A, 59E to Hove Park; time-limited free parking along Goldstone Crescent | Hours Always open | Tip Nearby Hove Park Café is a bustling place just a couple of minutes' walk north of the Goldstone, past the tennis courts. Catch the café in its charming 1925 appearance while you can. There are plans to replace it with a bigger, shinier structure

39__Hangleton Manor
One of the oldest buildings in town

If you fancy a nice traditional roast or superior tea and coffee in surroundings that may remind you of Harry Potter's Hogwarts, then Hangleton Manor is your place. It is a historical, architectural and culinary gem in the most unlikely of places: the outskirts of suburban Hove, and now entirely surrounded by 20th-century post-war residential buildings. You would not expect a fine 16th-century flint manor here, but the area is steeped in history. Hangleton village was first recorded in the 11th century and the manor is possibly the oldest domestic building in the city.

It was built for Richard Bellingham, twice Sherriff of Sussex, in the mid-16th century, but parts of it may be older. The long western block suggests an earlier building was incorporated into Bellingham's house, and carved stones from Lewes Priory (see ch. 103), demolished in 1538, have been found in the structure. For centuries it served as the operational centre of a large farm, which explains the row of cottages (possibly once stables) opposite, and the flint dovecote in the gardens. Other farm buildings were demolished in 1956 to make way for new roads and houses.

Hangleton Manor has many ingredients of a fine Tudor building, including large mullioned windows, a gabled porch, wood panels and screens, stone floors, fireplaces decorated with carved figures, and even a plaster ceiling with colourful heraldic emblems and beasts. The Commandment Room is particularly intriguing. It is so called because of versions of the 10 biblical commandments and proverbs carved into the beams and panelling. The room also has a very rare 'piscina', a wash basin sunk into the wall, possibly once used for communion service.

The manor is now run superbly by the Hall & Woodhouse family as a pub and restaurant and is for hire. You'd be advised to book a table if you are planning to come for a Sunday roast.

Address Hangleton Valley Drive, BN3 8AN, +44 (0)1273 413266, thehangletonmanor.co.uk, hangletonmanor.hove@hall-woodhouse.co.uk | Getting there Best reached by car via the A 293 turn-off from the A 27 bypass; 25-minute walk from Portslade Station; bus 59A, 66, 71, 71A to Hangleton Drive South | Hours Mon & Tue 11am – 10pm, Wed – Sat 11am – 11pm, Sun noon – 9pm; check website for food serving times | Tip The nearby parks and green spaces remind us of the ancient history of Hangleton. Just a few minutes' walk north-east of the manor is St Helen's Church, the medieval parish church of Hangleton, once the link between the manor and the village. The green stretch of land to the south of it was a 17th-century plague pit.

40 hiSbe Food
Join the supermarket rebels

Shopping for groceries needn't be boring, impersonal and ecologically unsustainable. Brighton's ethical shopping conscience is highly developed, but here is a relatively new supermarket that has taken sustainable consumerism to another level, packaging it with bright colours, snappy slogans and friendly customer service.

On the edge of the North Laine area, overlooking St Peter's Church green, sky blue doors invite you to enter hiSbe, short for How It Should Be: simple, good and sustainable. hiSbe is a Community Interest Company (CIC) that does business with the greater good of the local community and economy in mind. Sisters Amy and Ruth Anslow launched the first hiSbe Food store with their friend Jack Simmonds in 2013. They are self-proclaimed 'supermarket rebels' who have been challenging the overpowering presence of large supermarket chains. They consider the shop a social enterprise and champion a vision to 'smash Britain's out-of-date supermarket business model and reinvent a new kind'.

hiSbe offers seasonal fruit and vegetables and prioritises local Sussex produce in order to reduce food miles. If the latter isn't possible, the food has to be traceable, organic and free of chemicals. hiSbe is particularly committed to avoiding food and packaging waste. Dozens of staple foods and cleaning products are sold by weight, in paper bags or reusable bottles. Customers are encouraged to bring their own containers and bags for refills, or use the shop's compostable alternatives.

It could almost make you feel nostalgic, but there is nothing backward-looking about this shop. This is hopefully the new, ecologically-minded generation of supermarkets and consumers. Shopping for your groceries here will certainly make you feel good, and to make you feel even better there is a small café where you can have a rest before lugging your canvas bags home.

Address 20–21 York Place, BN1 4GU, +44 (0)1273 608028, hisbe.co.uk | Getting there 7-minute walk from Brighton Railway Station; many buses to St Peter's Church | Hours Daily 9am–8pm | Tip A few metres down the road, in St George's Place, is a splendid row of 14 bow-fronted Georgian town houses. Although in varying states of repair, the terrace gives you an idea of the elegance of the architecture that lined the way into Brighton from the north in the pre-railway age.

41 Hope & Harlequin

Dress like the Downton Abbey ladies

Hope & Harlequin is run by Louise Hall, whose background in fine art, jewellery design and interior decoration shines through in her choice of vintage and vintage-inspired women's dresses and accessories. If you need a really glamorous outfit or simply want to marvel at the shimmer and shine of yesteryear's fashion, this is the place.

After years of experience as a fashion buyer, Louise decided to set up her own business, specialising in high-end, original vintage clothes and vintage-inspired, made-to-order dresses. She covers the 1920s to 1970s and chooses her stock carefully, with emphasis on good-quality fabrics and wearability, but also often simply falling for a particular piece. There are usually spectacular examples of flowing event dresses in sumptuous colours on display. Louise also makes other pieces, ranging from silk camisoles and slips made from vintage parachute silk and antique lace trims, to customised cashmere.

Bespoke bridal wear is also one of Hope & Harlequin's specialities. Go to the far end of the shop and you will see a rail of gauzy, cream-coloured vintage wedding dresses, many of which could legitimately be added to a museum collection. Fittings take place in a quiet upstairs space, brimming with more beautiful vintage objects and clothes. Louise compares dresses to sculpture. This is apparent in her window displays, which often feature one single stunning vintage dress. Recently a local woman spotted her own wedding dress from 1975 in the window, remembering that she had sold it soon after she got married.

Celebrities and TV production companies often come to Hope & Harlequin looking for dresses from a specific period. In a Christmas special of *Downton Abbey* a few years ago, three of the Downton ladies were wearing original vintage dresses from this beautifully curated boutique in Brighton's Lanes.

Address 11 Ship Street Gardens, BN1 1AJ, +44 (0)1273 675222,
www.hopeandharlequin.com, shop@hopeandharlequin.com, bridal@hopeandharlequin.com |
Getting there 10-minute walk from Brighton Railway Station; many buses to Brighton
Station or North Road | Hours Mon 10.30am–6pm, Tue by appointment, Wed & Sat
10.30am–6pm, Sun 11am–5pm | Tip Just around the corner, in Middle Street, are two
historic landmarks of Brighton: The gorgeous Jewish synagogue, dating from 1875 and
occasionally open to the public, and the domed Hippodrome, where the likes of The Beatles
and The Rolling Stones once played. Shut and run down for years, it is awaiting restoration.

42_John Constable's House
'Piccadilly by the sea'

Two of the most popular British Romantic artists, J. M. W. Turner and John Constable, were part-time residents of Brighton and created great works inspired by the town. They came for different reasons, and with very different attitudes. Turner had a wealthy patron in Sussex, George Wyndham, 3rd Earl of Egremont, who had a villa in Brighton (now gone), where the artist probably stayed.

Constable, on the other hand, came to Brighton only reluctantly, without patronage. In 1824 his wife was in poor health, and it was thought that spending time by the sea would improve her condition. For the next four years the Constable family intermittently spent time in Brighton. Constable's reaction to the place was not favourable. In a letter to his friend Archdeacon Fisher from 29 May, 1824 he complains about the 'din and tumult', describing the town as 'a receptacle of the fashion and off-scouring of London … and the beach is only Piccadilly by the sea'. He nonetheless produced around 200 evocative oil sketches of the sea and the fields around Brighton. They are now among his most popular works.

Until recently it was not known where Constable stayed here. The letters gave his address as No. 9 Mrs Sober's Gardens, where he had set up a 'painting room', but the place could not be found. When the artist Peter Harrap bought a house in Sillwood Road in 2011, he was joined by local writer Shan Lancaster in finding out its story. Street names and house numbers had changed over the decades, but through meticulous research the mystery was finally solved, and 11 Sillwood Road was identified as the house where the Constables had lodged in the 1820s.

In 2013, a blue plaque was unveiled by Constable's great-great-grandson. And Peter Harrap must count himself the luckiest artist in the country, painting in the studio where the great Constable once worked.

Address 11 Sillwood Road, BN1 2LF | **Getting there** 20-minute walk from Brighton Railway Station; many buses to Waitrose in Western Road | **Hours** Not open to the public | **Tip** For coffee or lunch head two streets east to Preston Street, which is lined with restaurants of all types, and imagine Constable looking for a bite to eat nearly 200 years ago.

43   Kemp Town Tunnel

Alice's escape into Wonderland?

When star architects Busby & Wilds designed the astonishing Lewes Crescent for landowner and developer Thomas Read Kemp in the 1820s (see ch. 47), they made sure the Kemp Town Estate wasn't just bricks and mortar. The sea-facing, four-storey buildings of the Crescent and adjoining terraces and squares have no back gardens, but they surround nearly 15 acres of green space, the Kemp Town Enclosures. Envisaged by Kemp, they were designed by renowned botanist and landscape gardener Henry Phillips and surveyor Henry Edward Kendall in 1828, on the sloping land towards the sea, with shrubberies, trees and winding paths.

These gardens were communal, owned and cared for by the owners of the Kemp Town Estate houses, comprising Sussex Square, Lewes Crescent, Chichester Terrace and Arundel Terrace, and accessible only to them and their tenants. Now, as then, they are out of bounds to the general public, and a source of some mystery. When Phillips laid them out he also created at their southern end a tunnel, in order to provide private seafront access. It runs under what is now Marine Parade and emerges onto a terraced walk, flanked by two 'cottages', designed by Kendall, built into the wall, for a gardener and a policeman. Below is a 'Reading Room', where residents could relax.

You can walk along the esplanade, which is lovely in sunshine, but the tunnel is closed. Peep through the large iron gate, though, and you can see how it may have tickled writer Lewis Carroll's fantasy. He often stayed here with his sister, who lived at 11 Sussex Square, between 1874 and 1887. Some think that he included the intriguing ivy-covered tunnel in the opening scenes of his novel *Alice's Adventures in Wonderland*, in which Alice tumbles through a tunnel-like rabbit hole, but the book was published a decade earlier. Perhaps, though, the tunnel and the esplanade reminded him of Alice's world.

Address Kemp Town Enclosures, Marine Parade, BN2 1NB, kte.org.uk | Getting there 25-minute walk from the Royal Pavilion; bus 1, 1A, 7, 23 to Sussex Square, or 12, 12A, 14, 14A, 27 to Dukes Mound | Hours Closed to the public; esplanade always open | Tip A short walk west, below Dukes Mound, is Brighton Naturist Beach, the country's first public nudist beach. It opened in April 1980, following a campaign by local councillor Ellen Jakes, who faced strong opposition at the time. It is clearly demarcated and further protected from voyeurs or unsuspecting sensitive passers-by by large banks of shingle.

44 Kingston Buci Lighthouse

Lighting up Shoreham Harbour since 1846

At the western end of Shoreham Port (see ch. 75), at the mouth of the River Adur, is the site of the ancient Shoreham Harbour, recorded in Roman times as Portus Adurni. But there is also more recent history of significance here. Since the 1840s, a delightful lighthouse has been signalling fishermen to safety. It is known as Kingston Buci or Shoreham Lighthouse. The 13-metre-tall structure dates from 1842, despite the lintel saying 1846, the year it was first in operation. In 1850, the first lock was built in the eastern arm of the harbour, significantly increasing the amount of maritime traffic in the area. Kingston Buci replaced simple lanterns used as beacons and was built from local limestone and Caen stone imported from France, topped with an iron lantern roof.

The first rotating lantern was lit with oil lamps, which must have appeared rather weak by today's standards. In the 1880s these were replaced with a refracting glass gas lamp, operated by a mechanism like that of a longcase clock. In 1950, electric projector lamps were installed, creating a flash every 10 seconds, visible from 16 kilometres away. The lighthouse still operates, but no longer does a keeper have to climb 54 steps every day to wind up a clock mechanism. Timed light switches are now in place, cast-iron elements have been replaced with stainless steel, and the bronze ball and weather vane on the top have been restored. This fine lighthouse will probably guide boats into the safety of the harbour for decades to come.

For further protection of anyone in the sea near Shoreham, there has been a lifeboat in the harbour since 1865, and an RNLI lifeboat station is located near the lighthouse. The station is manned all year round by volunteers and welcomes visitors to take part in guided tours, or to see the memorabilia on display.

Address Shoreham Harbour Lifeboat Station, Kingston Beach, Brighton Road, BN43 6RN, +44 (0)1273 596376, www.shorehamlifeboat.co.uk, shoreham-lifeboat-visits@hotmail.com | **Getting there** 10-minute walk from Southwick Railway Station; 700 Coastliner to Lighthouse then 2-minute walk | **Hours** Not open to the public; lifeboat station: Mon–Fri 10am–2pm, Sat & Sun 10am–4pm | **Tip** A 10-minute walk away, by Shoreham Bridge, is the award-winning Ropetackle Arts Centre, a registered charity staffed by volunteers. It offers an impressive programme of live music, theatre, comedy and film, for audiences up to 350 strong (ropetacklecentre.co.uk).

45 Kipling's Gardens
Rottingdean's very own oasis

Rottingdean is a scenic half-hour bus ride away from the centre of Brighton. Bring a large bucket if you anticipate some serious crabbing in the rockpools at low tide. If it weren't for the relentless A 259 coast route traffic cutting through Rottingdean and separating it from its seafront, it could well be one of the most desirable villages in Sussex.

Rottingdean has many attractive medieval and Georgian buildings, an ancient church (see ch. 78) and perhaps one of the prettiest village greens in the country, complete with a pond where duckfeeding turns into an aesthetic experience. There are tasteful antique and designer shops, several reassuringly old-fashioned tearooms, as well as more contemporary coffee shops. In many ways, it is surprising that it is not completely overrun with tourists.

The beauty of Rottingdean's location was not lost on some big names in British literature and art. In large houses on the edges of the expansive green lived for many years the painters Edward Burne-Jones and later William Nicholson, and the author, journalist and traveller Rudyard Kipling, most famous for *The Jungle Book*. Kipling rented the 18th-century house, The Elms, on the north side of the green from 1897 until 1902, and it is where he wrote *Kim* and some of his *Just So Stories*. In 1902 he bought a more secluded and larger house in deepest Sussex, the 17th-century Bateman's at Burwash, where he lived until his death.

He may have deserted Rottingdean, but Kipling left us his beautiful gardens. The Elms itself is in private ownership and cannot be visited, but the adjoining ornamental gardens, complete with bee hives, picnic areas and a croquet lawn, have been open to the public since 1986. They are maintained with great care by Brighton Council, with support from the Rottingdean Preservation Company, which also looks after the nearby Rottingdean Windmill and Grange.

Address The Green, BN2 7HE, www.rottingdeanpreservationsociety.org.uk/the-kipling-gardens | Getting there Bus 2, 57, 84 to Rottingdean Pond or bus 2, 12, 14, 27, 47 to Rottingdean White Horse | Hours Daily 8am–dusk | Tip Walk around to the east wall of The Elms and try to find the 'wishing stone', a grotesque face of unknown date set into the flint structure. If you find it, stroke its nose, make a wish and then turn around three times to make it come true – but beware of the traffic!

46 Kissing Coppers and More
Brighton's most musical mural

There is much exciting street art in Brighton, but in 2004 the internationally famous British graffiti artist, Banksy, left his mark when he spray-painted a pair of policemen in a passionate clinch on the west wall of The Prince Albert pub near Brighton Railway Station. Brighton's annual Pride Festival has become one of the major LGBTQ+ events in the country, and *Kissing Coppers* seems a particularly poignant image to greet visitors, but it is also representative of the city's vibrant music scene.

Banksy, who has always kept his identity a secret, created the image soon after he started exhibiting in international galleries and Banksy-mania was just kicking off, and it became one of Banksy's most famous works. In May 2012 it was voted the most 'quintessentially British' work of art by other artists, in a poll carried out by The Other Art Fair in London. But not everybody approved of it: in 2006 it was vandalised in a paint attack. The pub landlord and his staff tried to clean and retouch the painting, but much of its original paint was lost.

In 2008, specialists were hired to remove the mural and replace it with a replica. Even this had to be protected from vandalism and was covered in Perspex. The original was flown to the USA in 2011 and there transferred onto canvas, in preparation for being sold at an auction in Miami in February 2014, where it made a respectable $575,000 (approx. £345,000). Like its creator, the buyer of the work decided to remain anonymous.

The coppers on the wall of The Prince Albert were in 2013 joined by a group of dead music icons, a large mural painted by artists Sinna One and Req One, among them John Lennon, Jimi Hendrix, Dusty Springfield and Amy Winehouse. David Bowie, Prince, George Michael, Ella Fitzgerald and Leonard Cohen have now joined them.

Address 48 Trafalgar Street, BN1 4ED | **Getting there** 2-minute walk from Brighton Railway Station; many buses to Brighton Station. Walk under the bridge down Trafalgar Street. You will see the Prince Albert immediately after the bridge on the corner of Frederick Place. | **Tip** The Prince Albert regularly offers live music and also serves traditional Spanish and Portuguese tapas. Staff here are famously friendly.

47 Lewes Crescent

Part of an unfinished masterpiece of urban planning

When you walk east along Marina Drive you pass glorious town-houses created at the height of Brighton's fame. They rise majestically with classical features and large windows. Rendered white or cream, it seems as if they are copying the chalk cliffs along the coast. The grandest Georgian structure of them all, at the eastern edge of the city, is the enormous Lewes Crescent, 28 four-storey houses arranged in a wide crescent shape, with huge private gardens at its centre (see ch. 43).

To either side are long terraces with more tall houses in the same style, while to the north the open crescent extends into Sussex Square, comprising 34 further houses. More terraces and squares were planned for this area known as Kemp Town, but only 106 of the 250 houses were actually built. Even in its truncated form, Kemp Town is the pinnacle of ambitious Georgian town planning, and Lewes Crescent is the jewel in this crown.

The man responsible was Thomas Read Kemp, a rich and influential Brighton resident who owned vast stretches of land in the area. He began developing this estate in 1823, clearly titillated by similar developments in Bath and London. With the help of architects Busby & Wilds and contractor Thomas Cubitt, who had built much of London's Belgravia and Pimlico, Kemp was trying to outdo them all. At a span of 256 metres, Lewes Crescent is 61 metres wider than the famous Royal Crescent in Bath, making it the is the largest residential crescent in Europe.

This was both vanity project and speculation: the houses, sold undecorated as empty shells, were aimed at the wealthiest of clients. William Cavendish, the 6th Duke of Devonshire purchased no.1 in 1829. It is now called Fife House, after a later owner, the Duke of Fife. Kemp eventually ran out of money and left the country in 1837 under financial pressures, while Cubitt bought many of the houses he had built here.

Address BN2 1FH, www.kemptownestatehistories.com/lewes-crescent | **Getting there** 25-minute walk from the Royal Pavilion; bus 1, 1A, 7, 23 to Sussex Square, or 12, 12A, 14, 14A, 27 to Dukes Mound | **Tip** Around the corner, at 9 Rock Street, is Busby & Wilds – not an architecture firm but a family-friendly, stylish gastropub with a back garden. The superb cuisine ranges from traditional English to Modern French, with roasts on Sundays. Good for a proper meal, or just a drink and a snack (busbyandwilds.co.uk).

48 London Road Viaduct

Rastrick's challenge: an indestructible bridge

The arrival of the railway in Brighton in the 1840s was an occasion of great significance (see ch. 13). After the London-Brighton line opened, visitor numbers increased dramatically, and the town expanded rapidly. It was not only the rail link that added to the business of the town, but also the Railway Engineering Works to the north of Brighton Railway Station, which looked after the railway stock and manufactured carriages and locomotives. By the 1890s, it employed more than 2,500 people.

Even before the main line opened, the London and Brighton Railway Act had authorised the creation of branches going west to Shoreham and east to Lewes and Newhaven. The line to Lewes opened in June 1846, with an intermediary stop at Falmer. The construction of the coast way branches was overseen by the inimitable railway architect John Urpeth Rastrick, whose huge tomb in the shape of a railway turntable in the Extra-Mural Cemetery (see ch. 26) is symbolic of his impact on Brighton.

Rastrick's challenge was the large steep-sided valley east of Brighton Railway Station, which could only be overcome by creating an artificial embankment or a viaduct. He decided on a viaduct, despite public criticism, and built the imposing, gently curving railway bridge to the north-east of the station. It is an eye-popping feat of Victorian engineering, and one of the largest viaducts in the country. Constructed with more than 10 million red and yellow bricks, it bridges the valley at a length of 370 metres. Its 27 spans reach a height of 20 metres. Astonishingly, it took only 10 months to build. Until the 1870s, the viaduct would have stood gloriously in open fields, but the city's expansion was unstoppable. It looks indestructible, but German bombs hit it in 1943, leaving the railway lines dangling in mid-air. However, it was repaired in record time. Look for slightly darker bricks to see the repairs.

Address Stretches east from Brighton Railway Station. Nearest postcode for the Preston Road site: BN1 4QG | Getting there 10-minute walk from Brighton Railway Station; bus 5, 5A, 17, 270, 271, 272, 273 to Springfield Road. Any trains going east will go over the viaduct and sometimes stop on it. | Tip A few steps north along Preston Road is the southern tip of Preston Park, where you find a scented rose garden with approximately 4,000 old-fashioned shrub roses and herbaceous borders, overlooked by the charming Rotunda Café, built in 1929.

49 Lucy & Yak
Colourful community clothing

If you would like to dress as colourful as Brighton itself, there is no better place than Lucy & Yak in the North Laine. It looks like a sartorial sweetshop, with brightly coloured, boldly patterned clothes lining the walls, all designed in Brighton. Muted tones and simpler patterns are also available, but for the full injection of Lucy & Yak positivity, you should probably consider the organic cotton dungarees in the Sunflower print. If you live in Brighton and are familiar with Lucy & Yak, expect to see their clothes popping up everywhere. This is a great example of a small, independent brand changing the look of a city.

But Lucy & Yak wants to change minds, too, and inspire people to make more sustainable and ethical choices The company was founded in 2017 by Lucy Greenwood and Chris Renwick, who in the years before had quit their jobs to travel the world. While in New Zealand, they started selling pouches sewn from recycled fabrics to fellow travellers. Later they sold vintage clothes from their beloved campervan named 'Yak'.

This kickstarted the idea of producing timeless, comfy, and practical clothes that could be part of a more sustainable fashion industry, where wages are fair, and there is transparency about where clothes were made and who made them. Their mission was to create a community that brings people together, through colourful, fun clothing, made of sustainable fabrics. 'Yaks', as they are affectionately known, are fairly priced and long-lasting, but if you are growing tired of or out of them, you can recirculate them: Used or imperfect Yaks can be resold, repaired or recycled through the Re:Yak Network.

Clearly, this is much more than a clothes shop or brand. Even Ed Sheeran loves Lucy & Yak, and has recently partnered with them on a collection of 'Sheerios' and 'Yakkers'. When asked what was most important to her about Lucy & Yak, Lucy said she wants the brand to encourage kindness, to be a welcoming place, a community.

Address 18 Kensington Gardens, BN1 4AL, +44 (0)7496690364, lucyandyak.com/pages/
our-shops-1 | **Getting there** 10-minute walk from Brighton Railway Station; 5-minute walk
from bus stops on or near the Old Steine | **Hours** Mon–Sat 10am–6pm, Sun 11am–6pm |
Tip Kensington Gardens is arguably one of the most exciting streets in the North Laine
area, with many quirky and independent shops. One of the greatest, quite literally, is
Snooper's Paradise, a sprawling flea market with more than 90 stalls. It has provided many a
Brighton reveller with clubbing and party outfits, as well as vintage furniture, crockery, and
vinyl records. snoopersparadise.co.uk

50_Madeira Lift

Victorian hydraulics take you to greater heights

Brighton has always had a problem with the sea claiming the land (see ch. 87). Erosion and landfalls were particular problems east of the Steine, where the chalk cliffs rise tall from the beach. In the late 18th century, Brighton wanted and needed to expand eastward, so developers made plans for a sea wall to protect the area from crumbling. In 1830, shortly after the Chain Pier had been built just south of what is now the Sea Life Centre, the engineer Thomas Cooper constructed a massive sea wall out of an early form of concrete. Over the decades the Victorians extended and strengthened both it and the eastern esplanades. At beach level, the east cliff road along the wall is called Madeira Drive, while the upper esplanade is known as Marine Parade. Then and now, these are the sunniest spots in Brighton, with far-reaching views over the sea.

Between 1889 and 1897, Borough Surveyor Philip Lockwood built the magnificent cast-iron Madeira Terrace, with balustrades and viewing platforms at upper levels and a continuous arcade, stretching 850 metres, along the foot of the wall. The arches are beautifully ornamented with keystones depicting Neptune and Venus, but have been neglected for many years. Parts of it are now in danger of collapsing and it is a race against time to save them. They look glorious, even in their sorry state of decay.

However, one part of the greater Madeira Terrace structure was recently restored: the lift linking Marine Parade with Madeira Drive at what is now the Concorde 2 live music club (originally a shelter hall). It opened in 1890 and was operated hydraulically, taking thousands of seaside visitors each year down to the beach or back up to street level. It now operates again during the warmer months, taking you straight inside the club. It gives hope that perhaps the council will succeed in restoring the rest of Madeira Terrace to its former glory.

Address Concorde 2, 286A Madeira Drive, BN2 1EN, +44 (0)1273 673311, www.concorde2.co.uk, hello@concorde2.co.uk | Getting there 15-minute walk from the Royal Pavilion; bus 12, 12A, 14, 27, 27B, 271, 272 to Burlington Street or Bedford Street | Hours The lift normally operates Easter to September 9.30am–7.30pm, but do check with Concorde 2 for details. | Tip If you walk along the eastern side of Brighton Pier, you get a good view of the Terrace and Madeira Drive. Imagine it as a fashionable equestrian promenade before the motorised age. At very low tide you can sometimes see remains of the 1823 Chain Pier's foundations below you.

51 Mae West's Lips
Salvador Dalí at his surreal best

Although an integral part of the Royal Pavilion Estate, Brighton Museum & Art Gallery has no royal origins. The building, whose style is in keeping with its neighbour, the Dome (built in the early 19th century as royal stables), was added in 1873, when the Pavilion had been in municipal ownership for a couple of decades. The museum is a proud example of Victorian public architecture, expressing the belief that having an art gallery was as important as good public transport or plumbing.

From modest beginnings the museum collections grew, comprising the fine and decorative arts, natural history, archaeology, world art and fashion (see ch. 29). The museum's Decorative Art collection is of national importance, and much of it is displayed in the central double-height gallery, where you can walk through the history of 20th-century art and design. Among the many superb pieces, a bright red sofa in the shape of a pair of lips stands out: one of the most iconic pieces of furniture ever designed and the work of the godfather of Surrealism, Salvador Dalí.

The sensual piece was the result of a collaboration between Dalí and his wealthy patron, the poet and collector Edward James, an avid supporter of Surrealism. In the 1930s he commissioned Dalí to create objects for the 'paranoiac-critical' interiors of Monkton House at his family's estate, West Dean in West Sussex. The sofa was one of these pieces, alongside the famous Lobster Telephone. It was designed in around 1938 and made by Green & Abbott. James and Dalí were probably inspired by a gouache Dalí had painted a couple of years earlier titled *Mae West's Face which May be Used as a Surrealist Apartment*. Five of the sofas were made, in slightly varying shades of red. It may be sensual and erotic, but it does not look comfortable. To be fair, Dalí never intended for it to be sat on. Visitors can try out a smaller version of it in the gallery.

Address Brighton Museum & Art Gallery, Royal Pavilion Gardens, BN1 1EE, +44 (0)1273 071273, brightonmuseums.org.uk/brighton, info@rpmt.org.uk | **Getting there** 15-minute walk from Brighton Railway Station; many buses to Old Steine or North Street | **Hours** Tue–Sun 10am–5pm, closed Mon (except bank holidays), 24 Dec (from 2.30pm) and 25 & 26 Dec | **Tip** In the warmer months there is no better place to enjoy tea, cake and sandwiches than in the outdoor Pavilion Gardens Café at the western edge of the Pavilion Gardens. From here you have a panoramic view of the Pavilion, the Dome and the Museum, while sitting under ancient trees. Beware of seagulls snatching your cake though (www.paviliongardenscafe.co.uk).

52 Marina
'Micro-Brighton' on the water

Curiously, it took Brighton until the 1970s to get a proper marina, despite technically having been a port for centuries. Located just east of Kemp Town (see ch. 43 and 47), near Black Rock, it is the largest complex of its kind in the UK, with a huge sea wall, a lock for the inner harbour and ample space for fishing, sailing, water sports and mooring, as well as more than 1,000 private homes, a large entertainment and retail area, hotels and restaurants.

What took so long? In the early years of the 19th century, a local civil engineer noted that flourishing Brighton was the 'largest place in Europe so near the seashore without a harbour or shelter for shipping'. Large ships could eventually dock at the Chain Pier, constructed in 1823, but over the next 140 years several plans for a designated harbour were ditched.

Concrete plans were made again in the 1960s, and Brighton got quite literally a mostly concrete harbour. It was officially opened to boats by Queen Elizabeth II in 1978, and marketed as 'Brighton's Cote d'Azur'.

The 1980s saw further developments in the form of housing, gigantic supermarkets, a multiplex cinema and bewildering concrete access roads and tunnels. More residential high-rise blocks were added recently, and a 40-storey tower block is planned.

Despite this continued investment and development, Brighton Marina is not an architecturally attractive place. It brims with restaurants and pubs, but most of them are chains. However, the location can't be argued with and it is a great place for alfresco dining. The family-run Master Mariner on the inner lagoon is the eatery with the most individual atmosphere. It serves locally sourced fish, beef, and a great Sunday roast. Watch the boats bobbing away in the water while enjoying your meal – the afternoon sun on the forest of masts is beautiful – or come for live music at weekends.

Address Security & Visitor Centre, Waterfront, Brighton Marina, BN2 5WA, +44 (0)1273 693 636, www.brightonmarina.co.uk | Getting there Bus 7 to Marina; free parking in the multi-storey car park | Hours Always accessible | Tip Every Sunday from 6am till 2pm the Brighton Marina Giant Car Boot Sale, Brighton's oldest and biggest boot fair, occupies the entire top floor of the multi-storey car park (www.brightonmarinagiantcarboot.co.uk).

53   Martha Gunn's Grave
A right royal dipper

The interesting graves in the churchyard of Brighton's ancient parish church St Nicholas of Myra (see ch. 56) include that of Nicholas Tettersall, who helped the future Charles II to escape to safety in France in 1651 (see ch. 61). One of the most beloved Brighton personalities entombed here is Martha Gunn. The inscription on her gravestone near the main entrance describes her as 'peculiarly distinguished as a bather in this town nearly 70 years'. But what kind of bathing could be a profession worth mentioning on a gravestone?

Gunn was born in Brighton in 1726, into a fishing family. She lived in a house near the Royal Pavilion (36 East Street) and died in 1815 at the age of 88, having worked her entire adult life as a bather. Bathers, also referred to as 'dippers', were strong, hardy people who would help anxious visitors who had come to Brighton to 'take the waters', into the sea.

Most of these health tourists could not swim. They changed into their swimming costumes in bathing machines (essentially huts on wheels that could be drawn into deeper water by donkeys), and from these they would take their plunge. Bathers like Martha Gunn would stand in the water and help them in and out of the sea.

You had to be of a particular physical type to do this kind of job, and large-framed Martha Gunn fit the bill. She also had rosy cheeks and a personality to match, it seems, and became something of a celebrity in Georgian Brighton, only retiring in her 80s. The Prince of Wales took a shine to her, and she was allowed access to the Royal Pavilion, including the kitchen areas. Another famous sea bathing professional – Sake Deen Mahomed, 'shampooing surgeon' to George IV – is buried nearby. He was one of the best-known early entrepreneurial Asian immigrants to Britain, and opened Mahomed's Baths near the seafront in 1812. His grave is on the north side of the church, visible but inaccessible.

In
memory of
STEPHEN GUNN
who died 4th of September 1813,
Aged 79 Years.
Also MARTHA, Wife of
STEPHEN GUNN,
who was Peculiarly Distinguished as a
bather in this Town nearly 70 Years.
She died 2nd of May 1815,
Aged 88 Years.
Also FRIEND, their Son

Address Church Street, BN1 3LJ, stnicholasbrighton.org.uk | Getting there 10-minute walk from Brighton Railway Station; many buses to Churchill Square | Hours Churchyard always open | Tip There are fine portraits of both Martha Gunn and Sake Deen Mahomed in Brighton Museum (see ch. 29 and 51), both depicted in rather smart costume. One of Mahomed's sumptuous Indian-inspired court dresses survives and is sometimes on display there, too.

54 Mills Fish Smokers
Serving fresh food and smiles

It is easy to forget that, before Brighton became an ultra-fashionable seaside resort in the mid-18th century, it had been a modest fishing town. Not many traces of the fishing industry are left. Although the Lanes area with the borders of North Street, East Street and West Street still has a recognisable medieval layout, you will be hard-pressed to find many original fishermen's cottages or any infrastructure relating to the fishing industry of the past.

However, just a few minutes west of Brighton Pier, perched on the beach just off the paved walkway at the bottom of the Kings Road Arches, stands a small black wooden structure, no bigger than a garden tool shed: a fully-operational, traditional smokehouse. It was built around the turn of the millennium by Jack and Linda Mills, and it is in here where freshly caught fish is smoked with oak and applewood, using only traditional ingredients and techniques. Smoking takes place almost daily and wisps of smoke can often be seen escaping from the hut. With its backdrop of the sea, and the groynes and piers in the middle distance, the smokehouse also makes a very attractive photographic motif.

Until their recent retirement, Jack and Linda used to sell their fish and seafood in arch opposite the smokehouse, next to the Brighton Fishing Museum (see ch. 12). The new owner continues the good work, and Linda still drops by. Colourful painted wooden signs and warm smiles invite you into the small space where time seems to have stood still. Here you get the freshest and most delicious crab or smoked mackerel sandwiches in town. In the summer months, mackerel is sometimes grilled on a barbecue outside, and in the winter fish soup is often on the menu. It is no wonder that this old-style 'smokers' with its simple and delicious food has been visited by many celebrity chefs and food critics, as well as politicians and journalists during the annual party conferences.

Address Kings Road Arches, BN1 1NB, +44 (0)1273 723064, www.brightonfishingmuseum.org.uk/quarter_fishsmokers.html | **Getting there** 15-minute walk from Brighton Railway Station; many buses to Churchill Square or Old Steine | **Hours** Daily, no specified opening times | **Tip** Take your hot mackerel sandwich and stroll a few hundred metres further west and look at the large-scale reconstruction work carried out at the 1880s Shelter Hall (150–154 Kings Road Arches), complete with a wooden kiosk on the upper promenade.

55 New Venture Theatre
Cutting-edge theatre in a haunted old school

The New Venture Theatre has been producing high-quality amateur theatre for many decades, and rarely gets the recognition it deserves.

The striking black-and-white building was originally a church school, built in 1841. Following the fire that destroyed the church in 1958, the school became the permanent home of the theatre company. It now has two performance spaces: a ground floor studio and the upstairs main theatre. The latter was recently completely refurbished, and productions now alternate between the two spaces. Beware: the upper floor is allegedly haunted, and many visitors have felt the sudden chill of a ghostly presence.

The NVT generally puts on no fewer than 10 productions per year. Anyone who wants to propose a play to direct can submit their suggestion for the following season. The current artistic director will make the selection, aiming for a good mixture of modern, classic and new writing. The NVT also holds other social events, as well as theatre workshops, play readings and acting classes.

The charitable organisation is entirely run by passionate volunteers, and operates a membership system, but you can of course just go to individual performances. Auditions are open to anyone and there is good 'cross pollination' between the NVT and other local theatre companies, so there is a steady influx of younger members from nearby universities.

The NVT team has created some extraordinary productions over the years. One of the most ambitious was Frank McCabe's adaptation of Charles Dickens' novel *Our Mutual Friend*, in 1998. It comprised two 2.5-hour acts, encompassed every acting and non-acting space in the building, and ran for two weeks with the acts alternating each night. The NVT doesn't feel amateur at all, and may just be the best place for exciting independent theatre along the south coast.

In case you were wondering, there is also a fully-licensed bar.

Address Bedford Place, BN1 2PT, +44 (0)1273 746118, www.newventure.org.uk, info@newventure.org.uk | Getting there 20-minute walk from Brighton Railway Station; many buses to Norfolk Square | Hours Performances all year, apart from August and September. Check website for details and performances. | Tip Just around the corner at 24 Sillwood Street is the Lion & Lobster, one of the oldest, cosiest and most traditional pubs in the city, serving excellent beer and food, with live music every Friday evening (www.thelionandlobster.co.uk).

56__Norman Font, St Nicholas

A superior medieval backrest

St Nicholas of Myra was the original parish church of the medieval village of Brighthelmstone. Old pictures show it perched high above the streets of the town, on a hill north-west of the Lanes. This elevated position was symbolic, as St Nicholas of Myra was the patron saint of sailors and fishermen, so the church was literally watching over Brighton.

The church appears smaller than it is, perhaps because it looks as if it has sunk into the soft chalky ground. It may just be the oldest building in Brighton, and is mentioned in William the Conqueror's Domesday Book from 1086, and there was possibly a church in this spot in Saxon times. It was greatly changed in the Victorian Age, but you can spot some medieval stonework at the base of the tower.

You get a real sense of the importance of St Nicholas' location when looking down towards the sea, despite the densely built-up areas now surrounding it. Inside, there is a gorgeous oak rood screen from the 15th century with a 19th-century makeover, but there is also one small but beautifully formed Norman object: a font that probably dates from 1170, made of French Caen stone. It is considered to be one of the best pieces of Norman carving in Sussex. It is older than the present church and may have a connection with the Priory in Lewes (see ch. 103).

The font has the shape of a circular drum and shows scenes from the New Testament – the Last Supper and the Baptism of Christ – and the life of St Nicholas. It is unclear what the fourth scene depicts. It wasn't always as highly regarded as it is now: sometime in the 17th century, wooden seating was installed around it and it was used as a bench, the fine carvings acting as backrests. It must have been quite uncomfortable, and caused visible damage to the figures. This is one of the few surviving objects that links Brighton's medieval history with the present.

Address Church Street, BN1 3LJ, stnicholasbrighton.org.uk | Getting there 10-minute walk from Brighton Railway Station; many buses to Churchill Square | Hours Churchyard: always open; church: Wed & Sat noon – 2pm; check website for services | Tip When you leave the church, continue south towards Churchill Square. Immediately to your left you will see a splendid example of residential Victorian 'Gothick', Wykeham Terrace. It looks like an elongated defensive castle, with castellated parapets and a grand gateway, and was possibly built by Amon Henry Wilds in the late 1820s (see ch. 91).

57 Old Police Cells Museum
The underbelly of the Town Hall

Brighton's Town Hall, built between 1830 and 1832 by Thomas Cooper, a town commissioner, is a proud building. It boasts porticos on two sides, with double-height columns in classical Doric and Ionic order, and sits a little awkwardly among the lower buildings in the medieval Lanes area of the former fishing village.

Enter through its main doors on the west side and you will see an attractive Italian mosaic floor, at its centre Brighton's coat of arms with stylised dolphins. However, the real surprise is beneath this pretty floor. In the basement is the town's original 19th-century police station, complete with 12 police cells, washrooms and store areas.

The basement served as the main Brighton police station from the founding of the force in 1838 until 1967. The cells date from the 1890s. The women detained here fared better than the men: their cells had wood floors and some daylight while the men's dark cells had stone floors. One weekend in 1964, when rivalry between 'Mods' and 'Rockers' turned violent, around 150 people were detained here, and some of their graffiti remains on the walls.

The museum is run almost entirely by volunteers, and many of the free tours are given by retired policemen who tell gripping stories about being 'on the beat'. The rooms are filled with photographs, memorabilia and police equipment, including a large collection of truncheons. A 3D-model used in court depicts the devastation caused by an IRA bomb that exploded in The Grand hotel in town during the 1984 Conservative party conference. It killed and injured many people and was the first attempt to wipe out the government since the Gunpowder Plot in 1605.

The police cells have recently been granted a wedding licence, so if you wanted to you could tie the knot behind bars, handcuffed to each other. Or you could just try on some police uniforms at the end of a tour.

Address Town Hall, Bartholomew Square, BN1 1JA, +44 (0)1273 901272, www.oldpolicecellsmuseum.org.uk, enquiries@oldpolicecellsmuseum.org.uk | Getting there 15-minute walk from Brighton Railway Station; many buses to Old Steine or North Street | Hours Tours usually available on Fridays and Saturdays, but phone or email ahead for details. | Tip The Grand hotel is only a short walk away. Head for the seafront, turn right and walk west for a few minutes and compare the restored white front of the 19th-century building to the model. The hotel is next to the 1960s' concrete Brighton Centre, where the party conference took place.

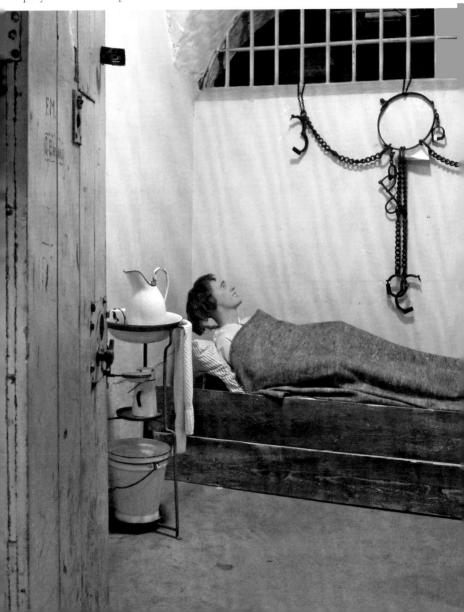

58__Oliver's Brighton

Where all your wizarding needs are met

Once a little rough around the edges, Trafalgar Street is now one of Brighton's most interesting streets, with an exciting array of independent businesses. One of these, unlike any other, is Oliver's Brighton, the brainchild of young entrepreneur Oliver Dall. Described as a 'mystical emporium for all your wizarding needs', it is a dreamlike vision of another world, where you may imagine you are in Victorian London rather than Brighton's North Laine. Naturally, this is where you come to buy yourself the perfect wand, and knowledgeable staff provide helpful advice.

The shop is beautifully designed. Oliver's aim was to create a retail shop with Victorian aesthetics (he kept the original beams and floorboards), a welcoming interior where customers feel intrigued and relaxed. All the furniture was sourced from Brighton antique shops, and bare vintage-style light bulbs illuminate the room. Oliver's rabbit, Luna Lepor, features in the shop's crest, and sometimes makes an appearance on the counter.

The products are carefully chosen, with a focus on quality, but there is something for every budget. Charms, for example, are available for just a few pounds, but you can also buy golden goblets, chocolate frogs, fantastical chess sets or an enchanted broomstick. On its opening day, 11 November, 2017, three-and-a-half-hour queues snaked down Trafalgar Street. It looks as if the hype won't be diminishing any time soon.

As well as an aesthetic vision, there is also strong moral spirit underpinning Oliver's business concept. Apart from a wealth of products relating to the world of magic, he has also created his own branded merchandise and donates £1 from each sale of these items, as well as voluntary donations for the shop's paper bags, to a local charity run by Jim Deans, supplying homeless people of Brighton with hot food every Sunday at the Clock Tower (see ch. 18).

Address 42 Trafalgar Street, BN1 4ED, +44 (0)1273 683439, www.oliversbrighton.co.uk, spell@oliversbrighton.co.uk | **Getting there** 3-minute walk (30 seconds on a broomstick) from Brighton Railway Station; many buses to Brighton Station | **Hours** Visiting is by appointment only | **Tip** According to Oliver, the best chai latte can be had at Milk No Sugar, a café opposite his shop that caters for vegans, vegetarians and those who are dairy and wheat intolerant (www.cafemilknosugar.com).

59 The Open Market
The spirit of Brighton under one big roof

Few places in Brighton brim with local life more than this colourful assembly of shops and stalls. The Open Market is the only covered market in Brighton and in the last few years has become much more than just a market.

Situated between London Road and Ditchling Road, halfway between the Level and Preston Circus, it has long been a place where Brighton people would flock to buy fresh fish from a real fishmonger, cheese, eggs, vegetables, bread and much more, at fair prices and from friendly traders. Until 2014, though, the market was a rather ramshackle assortment of semi-permanent stalls, and looked more than a little worse for wear. Tourists rarely came here. However, the market has always been a social hub and meeting place, and the council made the excellent decision to invest in its redevelopment.

It is now completely transformed: a solid cover was built; bright, colourful lights greet you at the entrances; and shops, studios and stalls are rented to passionate independent retailers and traditional market traders. There are dozens of retail units, selling everything you imagine: artisan bread, organic vegetables, vintage clothing, pet supplies, herbal remedies, flowers, spices, eggs, bacon, fish, leather bags, and many curiosities. The eateries are phenomenal: try, for example, delicious home-cooked Bangladeshi food at Spice of Life (Unit 19) while the Laptopchap at Unit 44 fixes your computer. There are also cafés and artists' studios under that big roof, as well as the popular community radio station, Radio Reverb, which broadcasts live from here every day.

During the week the market is calm and the perfect place for browsing. On Saturdays it erupts, with half the local population flocking to the temporary stalls in the centre. It is a place full of fun, warmth and creativity, and the perfect antidote to shopping malls.

Address Marshalls Row, BN1 4JU, +44 (0)1273 695728, www.brightonopenmarket.co.uk, info@brightonopenmarket.co.uk | Getting there 10-minute walk from Brighton or London Road Railway Station; many buses to Baker Street (London Road) or Open Market (Ditchling Road) | Hours Mon–Fri 9am–5pm, Sat 7am–5pm (stalls from 10am), Sun 10am–5pm | Tip The Open Market runs many family-friendly events, mostly at weekends, but also on some weekdays, such as live music, dance classes, pottery workshops, and outreach events for the local community.

60 The Other Sundial House

A house that tells time – on a sunny day

There is a large house boasting a lovely sundial on its south wall right in the centre of Brighton, on the corner of Queen's Road and North Road, called Sundial House. However, there is another, less obvious Sundial House in Brighton, of perhaps greater interest to sundial enthusiasts. In Upper Lewes Road, an area known for its thriving student population, a private terraced house has been turned by its owner, Jackie Jones, into one large, personalised sundial.

'Dialist' Jackie grew up in Greenwich and, perhaps unsurprisingly, became fascinated with sundials from an early age. Having spent much time in the National Maritime Museum and the Observatory, she became familiar with their history and use. When she moved to Brighton, she noticed her house had an obvious recess for a dial above the front door and decided to make one. Involved with the British Sundial Society, she understood how to accurately set out the hour lines. A painted dial seemed a good idea, and after creating meticulous plans she hired a scaffolding frame and started the work with her husband, Rob Stephenson.

The house faces roughly south-east and the dial shows the hours and half-hours from early morning until just after 2pm. The hour lines contain a Morse code message: EQUALITY. The curved lines crossing them mark the equinox, summer and winter solstices. A red line incorporated in the design marks Jackie and Rob's wedding anniversary. On these dates the shadow of the round bead on the gnomon tracks these lines. The gnomon was made by Jackie of brass and gilding metal, with a silver bead for a nodus.

A jeweller by profession, Jackie has also created sundials made of silver, paper, card and other materials, and has even printed them on drinking glasses – for those who are keen, and not too inebriated, to adjust their pint of beer correctly while enjoying a sunny afternoon.

Address 51 Upper Lewes Road, BN2 3FH, diallist.wordpress.com/jackie-jones | Getting there 10-minute walk from London Road Railway Station; bus 23, 24, 25, 37, 48, 49, 74, 78 to Melbourne Street | Hours Not open to the public | Tip Walk around 150 metres west on Upper Lewes Road and turn into Round Hill Crescent, then look out for the 'Cat Creep', a 160-step stairway connecting the Crescent to Richmond Road. It is allegedly the steepest thoroughfare in the city.

61 Paganini Ballroom

Dance like Jane Austen

The Old Ship Hotel, which occupies almost the entire length of King's Road between Ship Street and Black Lion Street, is one of the oldest buildings in Brighton. Its sea-facing façade looks rather plain compared to the grand Victorian hotels nearby, but its history is illustrious.

It started life in the mid-16th century as a small Tudor inn in Ship Street. In 1671 it was bought by Captain Nicholas Tettersell, with money he received from helping King Charles II escape to France from Shoreham (see ch. 45, 75 and 79). Adjoining houses were slowly bought up and incorporated, gradually creating a sea-facing front. In the mid-18th century, the Tudor structure was completely remodelled, and in 1761 assembly rooms were added in a classical style, including an additional ballroom, complete with a royal box and a musicians' balcony.

Every seaside resort of note had to have such a ballroom, as dancing and music lay at the heart of Georgian social life. Jane Austen, who may well have visited Brighton and describes its temptations with great wit in her novel *Pride and Prejudice*, loved dancing and regularly attended balls at assembly rooms with her sister, especially when staying in seaside resorts. A fair amount of flirting appears to have gone on and she clearly found rich material for her writing at balls. If indeed Austen came to Brighton, she probably danced here.

Brighton had two assembly rooms, at the Castle Inn on the Steine, abutting the Royal Pavilion, and the one at the Old Ship. The Castle Inn is long gone, but the Ship rooms survive, and are still used for dances, concerts and special events. George IV frequented the Ship's assembly rooms, as did his brother William IV. The additional ballroom is now called the Paganini Room, after the famous violinist Niccolò Paganini, who played on the balcony to a mesmerised audience on 9 December, 1831 and stayed the night at the hotel.

Address King's Road, BN1 1NR, +44 (0)1273 329001, www.thecairncollection.co.uk/hotels/the-old-ship, reservations@oldshipbrighton.co.uk | **Getting there** 5-minute walk from the Royal Pavilion; many buses to Old Steine or North Street | **Hours** Hotel always open, but you need to ask whether it is possible to see the historic rooms | **Tip** On the Ship Street side look for the doorframe of the original entrance to the hotel, before it was moved to the King's Road side in the 1840s. The Hotel du Vin opposite (once called the New Ship, just to confuse matters) serves great Sunday lunches and has a refined wine list (www.hotelduvin.com/locations/brighton).

62 Park Crescent Gates

Where exotic creatures used to roam

Just north of the Level lies Park Crescent, a horse-shoe shaped range of 48 residential buildings, designed and built between 1849 and 1854 by Amon Henry Wilds (see ch. 26, 47, 81 and 91). It is one of the last examples of elegant Italianate-style terraces that had become popular in the Georgian period. The Crescent encloses a large private garden only accessible to residents. A pair of stone lions adorn the top of the gate columns. Why?

Before it became a fashionable address, the land was bought by entrepreneur James Ireland, who in 1822 opened Ireland's Gardens, a landscaped pleasure garden including a cricket ground, ball room, grotto, aviary, maze and other attractions. They were never quite finished, however, and Ireland sold them after a few years.

Inspired by London's Zoological Gardens, attempts were made to establish a zoo in Brighton. It was on the site of Ireland's Gardens that the establishment of the Royal Zoological Gardens was dreamed up in the early 1830s. A print shows what was envisaged but never completed: an assembly of vaguely oriental structures, typical of 18th-century pleasure gardens and 19th-century zoo architecture.

Although these designs were never fully realised, the place was soon advertised as 'Zoological Gardens'. In an 1833 book about Sussex, J. D. Parry writes: 'The collection of animals is at present small […] It consists of two young tigers, two fine leopards, a panther, hyaena, a lynx, two Russian bears, foreign goats, deer, lamas, monkeys, &c. &c. The lion and the elephant are still wanting. A boa constrictor is the only curiosity of that class. There is a beautiful assortment of birds, paroquets, cockatoos, macaws, &c.' The grounds closed in 1833. Of the zoo's architecture, only the lion gate survives, a reminder of Brighton's ambitious past. One wonders how many Park Crescent residents know they are walking on the remains of one of the earliest zoos in Europe.

Address Park Crescent, Round Hill, Brighton, BN2 | **Getting there** 15-minute walk from Brighton or London Road Railway Station; many buses to Elm Grove | **Tip** The aptly name Park Crescent Pub, tucked away at the back of the Crescent, is so cosy it makes you feel you have stepped into someone's living room. Serves good food, too, including Sunday roasts (theparkcrescent.co.uk).

63__Pepper Pot

Remains of a glorious villa

One of the most curious buildings in Brighton, beloved and neglected in equal measure, is the Pepper Pot, also known as the Pepper Box, in a residential area just north of Queen's Park.

The elegant, white, cylindrical tower stands 18 metres tall and is a complex design comprising an octagonal plinth, on which sits a circular corniced level surrounded by 11 Corinthian columns, topped with another level of shorter pilasters and a final cupola with a copper finial. There are two rows of small windows on the upper level and one large door at the base, but it does not look like a domestic dwelling. Despite its funny nickname it is a very elegant building, designed in 1830 by the famous architect Sir Charles Barry, best known for rebuilding the Houses of Parliament, but despite these credentials we know little about its intended use, and many myths have evolved around it. Some people believe it was a smuggling site, with secret tunnels leading to the seafront.

What we do know is that it is the only complete structure surviving of the buildings that were part of a magnificent villa built for Thomas Attree, one of the movers and shakers of Georgian Brighton. As a young man he started working for his father's law firm, Attree & Son, and later was responsible for much of the legal work concerning the Royal Pavilion. A very rich man, he bought and developed several large estates in Brighton, including Queen's Park, where he built his stylish villa, one of the earliest examples of the Italianate style in the country.

The Pepper Pot may have been an observation or water tower for the villa, or just possibly a folly. Inexplicably, the Attree Villa was demolished in 1972, with only the Pepper Pot a reminder of its classical splendour. After Attree's death, the tower was used for many purposes, including as the place where the *Brighton Mail* was published and printed.

Address Tower Road, BN2 0FZ | Getting there 20-minute walk from the Royal Pavilion; bus 18, 23, 37B, 74, 94A to Pepper Pot | Hours Not open to the public, but free to walk around | Tip Wander into Queen's Park, now a public space, and look for other relics of Thomas Attree's villa in and around the edges of the park. You will find some old walls, a gatepost, a gazebo-like structure and parts of the villa's garden temple.

64 Percy & Wagner Almshouses

A philanthropic memorial with a link to Washington

At the bottom of Elm Grove, partly shielded by large trees, is a row of 12 pretty two-storey cottages. Their appealing Gothic features give them 'a sense of stability', noted an 1821 Brighton handbook. Originally almshouses for poor Anglican widows, offering them shelter, a small income and clothing, they have little-known stories to tell.

Almshouses were relatively common in affluent towns in the 18th and 19th centuries, but these ones are quite special. Originally there were only six, built in 1795. In 1859, the influential and philanthropic Vicar of Brighton, Henry Michell Wagner (see ch. 82), with his sister Mary, added three to either side, intended for 'poor maidens'.

A more intriguing story concerns the first six cottages (nos 4–9). The inscription under the eaves reads: 'These Almshouses were erected and endowed at the request of the late Philadelphia and Dorothy Percy AD 1795'. When these sisters died in their early twenties, their mother, the respected widow Margaret Marriott, arranged for the cottages to be built as a memorial. The girls were not Mrs Marriott's late husband's children, but the illegitimate offspring of Hugh Percy, 1st Duke of Northumberland. This was public knowledge – the girls even took their father's surname – and did not seem to have damaged Mrs Marriott's reputation in society.

The girls' half-brother, James Smithson – another of the duke's illegitimate offspring, became an internationally renowned chemist. He decreed that after his death his wealth should be used to create 'an establishment for the increase and diffusion of knowledge' in the United States. This is the famous Smithsonian Institution in Washington, which links these modest almshouses with one of the greatest museums and research centres in the world.

The almshouses were restored and enlarged in 1975.

Address 1–12 Islingword Road, BN2 9SW | Getting there 15-minute walk from Brighton or London Road Railway Station; many bus routes to Elm Grove | Hours The almhouses are not open to the public, but can easily be viewed from the north and west. Please respect the owners' privacy. | Tip In the collection of Brighton Museum is the only known portrait of Mrs Marriott, looking elegant, and slightly melancholy. It was painted by one of the superstars of the European art scene at the time, Angelica Kauffman, who had come from Austria to carve out a glittering career at the newly founded Royal Academy in London.

65 Pet Cemetery

Preston Manor graveyard for beloved dogs and cats

Preston Manor is a fascinating historic manor house on the north-ern outskirts of Brighton. It has 13th-century origins, was rebuilt in the early 18th century, greatly enlarged in the early 20th century and is now decorated and furnished in elegant Edwardian style. In 1932 its last owners, the Stanford family, bequeathed it to the town of Brighton and it is now a beautiful museum. Allegedly haunted, Preston Manor has many surprises in store, including a charming pet cemetery, where many a Victorian and Edwardian pooch and kitten found its last resting place.

Dogs were clearly especially important to the Preston Manor own-ers, and almost considered family members, reflected in numerous dog portraits that hang in prominent position in the house. Some, if not all, of these loyal companions were buried by the south wall of Preston Manor Garden, a beautiful walled garden to the south-west of the house. Some were given tiny gravestones with endearing inscriptions. They are now badly weathered and can be hard to spot among the vegetation in high season, but look carefully and you will see, for example, one to 'Jock. Stout of Heart and Body 1911–1919'. Kylin, Lady Thomas-Stanford's Pekingese, is remembered as being 'Faithful and Fearless 1909–1924'. Another one is inscribed to 'my Dear and Faithful Dog Pickle my Constant Friend and Companion for 14 years'. The most intriguing stone dates from 1884 and tells us of 'Dear Soot who for 9 years was our faithful Friend and Playfellow who was cruelly poisoned.'

Fortunately, we know some of the background stories through a collection of articles written in 1935 by Margery Roberts, daugh-ter of the Manor's curator, for the *Sussex Daily News*. She tells us of Peter, a Scotch terrier 'who bit everyone in a white apron'. His tiny gravestone reads: 'In Memory of Dear Peter, who was cross and sulky but loved us'.

Address Preston Manor, Preston Drove, BN1 6SD, +44 (0)1273 071273, brightonmuseums.org.uk/prestonmanor, info@rpmt.org.uk | Getting there 10-minute walk from Preston Park Railway Station; bus 5, 5A to Preston Drove, then 2-minute walk | Hours 25 April–27 May, Sat & Sun 10am–5pm; check website for additional seasonal opening times | Tip On the other side of Preston Road is Preston Park Rockery, allegedly the largest municipal rock garden in the country, created in 1936 on an overgrown railway bank.

66_Portslade Brewery

Magnificent industrial architecture

Portslade is one of several ancient Downlands villages that are now part of greater Brighton. While slightly off the beaten track, they all have fascinating histories and are worth visiting. In most of them you find medieval parish churches and lovely examples of flint-fronted cottages, which give you an idea what Brighton might have looked like when it was a fishing village.

Portslade village is approximately 1.6 kilometres inland, possibly on the line of a Roman road that ran from London to the port at Shoreham (see ch. 75). It retains some of its medieval street pattern and boasts a 12th-century church, St Nicolas, which abuts the Emmaus centre (see ch. 24). Among the pretty old cottages and low houses that line its streets is one building complex that stands out in respect of height and design: the old Portslade Brewery with its tall chimney.

A brewery was first recorded on the site in 1789. The area was known for its superior water, making the establishment of a brew house a lucrative enterprise.

The surviving five-storey brewery building dates from c.1881 and was built for John Dudney. It was one of the largest breweries in Sussex and was then described as looking 'cathedral-like amid the cottages'. It still does, and its tall chimney with a colourful plaster vignette at its base, bearing the initials D&S (for Dudney & Sons), quickly became a landmark. The yellow-brick brewery and its nearby mid-19th-century malthouse with its attractive pyramid roof are now Grade-II listed buildings.

The nearby pebble-fronted Stag's Head pub and other buildings were once part of the greater brewery complex, and there are rumours of tunnels between the pub and the brewery cellars. The brewery has seen many owners, including the Mews Brothers, Smithers, Tamplin's, Shepherd's Industries and Le Carbone. The site is now awaiting possible conversion into flats.

Address North side of High Street, Portslade, BN41 2LG | **Getting there** Best reached by car, or bus 1, 1A to St Nicolas Church, Portslade | **Hours** Not open to the public, but free to walk around | **Tip** Look out for work by the local Surrealist painter Barrie Sydney Huntbach (1935–2006) in Portslade. You find a large three-panel painting, *The Return of the Prodigal Son* (1971), in the main function room of the Town Hall (check opening times online), and another one in the Superstore of Emmaus (see ch. 24).

67   The 'Preston Twins'

Gilded glory for ancient elm trees

Probably no tree plays a greater role in British culture and history than the English elm (*Ulmus minor* var. *vulgaris*). Sadly, the elm population in Britain has been in steady and catastrophic decline since the early 1970s, with many mature trees falling victim to Dutch elm disease. Miraculously, and despite great losses during the Great Storm of 1987, the area of Brighton and Hove hosts the largest surviving population of these magnificent trees. Whilst not entirely immune to the disease – the Pavilion Gardens recently lost a large specimen – the city boasts around 17,000 English elms, thanks to the council's immediate action to control the spread of disease.

Most of Brighton's elms were planted in the 19th and early 20th centuries and can be found in significant numbers on the Level, in Preston Park and other parks, along Dyke Road and the Old Shoreham Road, in the surrounding countryside, and even in private gardens. They are not just beautiful trees but important ecosystems: the population of the elm-dependent rare butterfly, the White-letter Hairstreak butterfly, rises and falls with the trees.

The two specimens at the north end of Preston Park were extra-special. Each with a girth of nearly seven metres, they were thought to be more then 400 years old, and possibly the oldest elms in the world. One of the 'Preston Twins' recently succumbed to extreme weather and Dutch Elm disease, but will soon return as a work of art: sculptor Elpida Hadzi-Vasileva has carefully preserved and gilded the hollow trunk of the elm, and from 2022 it will join its twin again. Brighton & Hove council is keeping a very close eye on the surviving twin. It is checked for disease and pruned regularly, as the weight of the canopy could cause it to collapse. Just imagine: when these trees were planted, Shakespeare was alive, Queen Elizabeth I was ruling Britain, and Brighton was still around 150 years away from becoming a popular bathing place.

Address Lime Tree Walk, BN1 6DT | **Getting there** 10-minute walk from Preston Park Railway Station; bus 5, 5A to Preston Drove then 2-minute walk. The elms can easily be seen and approached from Preston Road. Enter Preston Park from its western side at Lime Tree Walk. | **Hours** For more information on the Preston Park Gilded Twin project see: www.elpihv.co.uk/works/preston-park-gilded-twin | **Tip** The Chalet Café is situated nearby at the centre of Preston Park and is particularly good for people-watching in the summer.

68 The Regency Town House

Includes a time capsule of the servants' world

Very few of the grand Regency houses in the city have escaped conversion into flats. This grade I-listed terraced house, built in the mid-1820s, is one of these exceptions. For more than 25 years, Nick Tyson and his team of volunteers, interns and students have been developing it as a heritage centre and museum. Supported by The Brunswick Town Charitable Trust, it is slowly being restored to its original splendour. The Town House also offers opportunities to find out more about the conservation of historic houses and the social history of the city between 1780 and 1850.

There is little furniture in the main drawing rooms on the first and second floors yet, but the early decorative schemes of the building have been accurately recreated, and many architectural features survive. Multiple layers of paint and wallpaper have been revealed, some of them imitating stone or marble. The large rooms provide space for the many events taking place here, including lectures, art exhibitions, concerts and themed dinners.

The Regency Town House has another surprise up its sleeve: in 1995 the servants' basement of 10 Brunswick Square was acquired and now forms an annexe to the museum. It had been lived in for many years by an elderly lady whose parents had been housekeepers at numbers 9 and 10. The space had never been fully modernised and retained many original features, including a housekeeper's room, wine cellar, butler's pantry, servants' hall, ice larder, meat safe and vaulted coal stores. The locks of the wine cellar were still sealed with wax.

When the lady moved out, the team had only three months to raise the money to buy it. Generous donations from the general public and the first ever Heritage Lottery Fund grant in the South East made the purchase possible. Years of restoration work followed, during which an original well was unearthed.

Address 13 Brunswick Square, BN3 1EH, +44 (0)1273 206306, rth.org.uk, office@rth.org.uk | Getting there 25-minute walk from Brighton Railway Station; many buses to Brunswick Place | Hours No specific hours. The Regency Town House offers fully-guided tours of the main house and the basement in the warmer months of the year, or on request. Check website or Facebook page, or subscribe to email list for guided tours, open days and events. | Tip For the best view of a sweeping Georgian crescent facing the sea, walk a bit further west along the seafront until you see Adelaide Crescent (originally designed by Decimus Burton), with its magnificent double-s-shaped layout.

69__Resident

A music shop good enough for Nick Cave

Brighton's music scene is exciting and cutting edge, with many venues of all sizes putting on events all year round. Each May, The Great Escape festival showcases more than 400 new acts in over 30 venues across the city. No wonder then that music shops are doing well here. The arrival of digital streaming and the overpowering presence of online retailers made a dent in the number of independent shops, but a few have come out bigger, stronger and better, offering what online retailers can't – personality, passion, carefully curated stock, and live music.

Resident is one of these superior independent enterprises. Located right at the centre of the North Laine area, it has established itself as a much-loved and respected music shop. Even local music royalty Nick Cave is a fan and customer. In 2019 Resident was named Best Independent Retailer at the prestigious Music Week Awards.

Resident was opened by husband-and-wife team Derry Watkins and Natasha Youngs in 2004 in this prime location. Eleven years later they expanded, incorporating the shop next door, which means it now has an open, sprawling feel, without feeling crammed. They have a team of a dozen staff, all extremely knowledgeable and friendly, and happy to have a chat about music. You can buy tickets for local gigs here, too, and Resident also puts on their own gigs in the shop.

On the shop floor you will find an equally weighted selection of vinyl and CDs, covering rock, indie, country, hip-hop/R&B, folk, blues, world, reggae, metal, soundtracks, 'Out There' and dance/electronica. There are listening posts and excellent descriptions and reviews of new releases, published online (their website is a cut above!) and in a free magazine, the *Resident Annual*, in which staff choose their favourite records of the year, and write about them. It is the human interaction that makes this shop so special.

Address 28 Kensington Gardens, BN1 4AL, +44 (0)1273 606312, www.resident-music.com,
info@resident-music.com | **Getting there** 10-minute walk from Brighton Railway
Station; many buses to North Street or Old Steine | **Hours** Mon–Sat 9am–6.30pm, Sun
10am–6pm | **Tip** Each year around Easter, Resident takes part in Record Store Day, an
international event to celebrate the culture of record shops. For the occasion, Resident orders
pretty much every newly released record in the country, provides track listings and info, and
puts on special events. See website for details.

70__Royal Crescent
Classy enough for acting royalty

Brighton boasts some of the best Georgian architecture in the country, reflecting its meteoric rise in popularity as a 'watering place' from the 1740s onwards. If you find yourself walking towards the eastern edge of the city, look out for this architectural gem.

Located halfway between the Pier and Kemp Town, on the eastern cliffs of Brighton, this crescent of 14 terraced houses may well be the first example in the city of this type of elegant Georgian structure. Unfortunately, little is known about its origins, but it was built by the merchant and speculator J. B. Otto between c.1796 and 1805, to designs by an unknown architect. Otto clearly tried to impress the Prince of Wales, and at one point erected a statue of him on the lawn, which crumbled within a few years.

The terrace is built in an east to west alignment, with the first and last house being parallel to the seafront and the others forming a gentle shallow curve. This means that each house has direct and full views of the sea. It is easy to forget that in the first few years this crescent would have stood almost on its own, in open country, at a short but safe distance from all the noise of the town.

The Royal Crescent has particularly beautiful porches, doorways and canopied verandas, which create a unified style, and is a great example of Sussex 'mathematical tiles' (see ch. 94), here glazed in black. On a sunny day, the reflection of the tiles in combination with the gleaming white doors and window frames make for a stunning vision.

This type of permanent or seasonal residence was extremely popular with the wealthy middle and upper classes, and would have been considered the height of fashion. It has remained one of the most popular addresses of Brighton and has seen several famous residents, among them the theatrical couple Sir Laurence Olivier and Joan Plowright, who owned numbers 5 and 6 in the 1960s and 1970s.

Address Royal Crescent, BN2 1AL | Getting there 25-minute walk from Brighton Railway Station, or a leisurely 10-minute walk east from Brighton Pier; bus 12, 12A, 14, 27 to Bedford Street South | Hours Not open to the public | Tip A 5-minute walk away, at 33 Upper St James's Street, is the Hand in Hand, a microbrewery pub where you can enjoy 'mainly beer, mostly beer and nearly always beer', and some of it made on site (www.handbrewpub.com).

71 Royal Pavilion North Gate
Fraternal competition – in the most romantic way

You can't but marvel at the exotic beauty of the Royal Pavilion (see ch. 22), but it is worth looking at other wonders on the estate, such as the magnificent and underappreciated North Gate. You may think it is also by John Nash and commissioned by George IV, as it is so similar in style to the Pavilion, but this is the work of architect and surveyor Joseph Henry Good, and was built in 1832, in the early years of the short reign of George IV's successor, his brother William IV. A party animal like George, William had great plans for the pleasure palace by the sea and engaged Good to add numerous buildings, including splendid gates at the north and south entrances. The South Gate does not survive. We don't know exactly how the gates looked before Good, but in Nash's ground plan from 1826 they are shown as very small square structures, perhaps in the style of sentry boxes.

Good came up with around 45 proposals for the North Gate alone. His architectural plans survive and show how he played with a range of exotic and essentially Romantic ideas, including cladding the gate in blue and white tiles. The winning design is a well-proportioned, grand symmetrical gate with a central arch, minarets and a copper dome, which has turned a shimmering green.

This proud building would have been one of the first glimpses of the Pavilion estate for Brighton visitors approaching from the north, and is still the first structure you see when you arrive by bus from Lewes or by car from London Road. Although a bit weathered on the south side it looks attractive at any time of the day and year, whether framed by barren elm trees in winter, or by hollyhocks and other colourful flowers in spring and summer. It looks particularly beautiful with sunshine on its southern side at mid-morning or late afternoon. It now appropriately houses the offices of the estate's Head Gardener and his volunteers.

Address 120 Church Street, BN1 1AU | **Getting there** 3-minute walk from Old Steine; many buses to Old Steine or North Street | **Hours** The North Gate is not open to the public, but the surrounding gardens are open 24 hours. | **Tip** Immediately to the west of the North Gate is North Gate House, with a gleaming white orientalised façade. One of a row of late-18th-century townhouses, all of which were bought by the Prince of Wales to develop his estate, this is the only one that wasn't demolished. It is now part of Brighton Museum (brightonmuseums.org.uk).

72 The Royal Pavilion Tunnel
Secret escape route for a king?

Brightonians love a secret tunnel, and many urban myths are circulating about tunnels from Regency terraces to the sea (see ch. 43) and from the Royal Pavilion to George IV's illegal wife Maria Fitzherbert's house on the Old Steine. Some of these tunnels are fantasy, but some do exist, and one can be spotted with the naked eye if you look carefully.

A so-called 'cut-and-cover' tunnel runs north-west from the north end of the Royal Pavilion – the last part of the palace to be finished in the early 1820s – to the king's former stables (now the Dome concert hall).

Referred to as a 'subterranean passage' in the cost proposal dated 10 December, 1821, the tunnel was constructed in the last stages of the oriental transformation of the palace and its grounds that had begun in 1815 under the guidance of the famous architect John Nash. It cost £1,783 to build and was constructed with bricks, cement, clay and an unreliable material called 'mastic', and was lit by circular glass lights sunk into its arched ceiling. This trail of 8 top lights, some containing the original 1821 glass, can be traced in the flower beds and paths of the Pavilion grounds. At its highest point the tunnel measures just 2.6 metres and you can just about spread your arms out in it. There are recesses for gas lights, and many evocative holes and markings on the walls.

In 2013, extensive restoration work was carried out on the tunnel, mainly to strengthen it and make it safe to open it to the public. The work helped in understanding the tunnel better, but there are still many unanswered questions: why exactly was it built and who used it? Could the ailing king really have made it down a spiral staircase and through a narrow tunnel to get to his horses? Was it perhaps for bringing messy goods into the palace without disturbing the newly laid-out Regency gardens?

Address The Royal Pavilion, 4/5 Pavilion Buildings, BN1 1EE, +44 (0)1273 071273, brightonmuseums.org.uk/royalpavilion, info@rpmt.org.uk | Getting there 3-minute walk from Old Steine; many buses to Old Steine or North Street | Hours Royal Pavilion daily Oct–Mar 10am–5.15pm, Apr–Sep 9.30am–5.45pm. Tunnel tours only run on selected dates throughout the year and are strictly limited. Please check the website or ask at the front desk for details. | Tip When looking for the tunnel top lights in the ground, take time to appreciate the flora and fauna in the Pavilion Gardens. The Regency-style garden is maintained by Head Gardener Rob Boyle, his team, and his volunteers, who will happily chat with you about ancient elms, exotic plants and rare birds and butterflies.

73 Sassoon Mausoleum
No bodies left here, just exotic vibes

In the heart of Kemp Town, Brighton's 19th-century eastern development (see ch. 43 and 47), is a single-storey building that looks like an outpost of the Royal Pavilion. From behind stark, windowless walls with only one scalloped entrance, a circular tent-shaped copper roof rises from the corner of St George's Road and Paston Place. It was clearly inspired by the roofs of the Pavilion's Banqueting and Music Rooms, but the creator of this one originally outdid the spectacle of the Pavilion by covering the roof in gold leaf.

The structure was built as a mausoleum in 1892 by someone who had perhaps a little more reason to refer to Middle Eastern and Indian styles: the immensely rich philanthropist Sir Albert Abdullah David Sassoon, who was born in Baghdad, modern-day Iraq, in 1818 into a Sephardic Jewish family of bankers and merchants. After settling in Bombay (now Mumbai), he founded large businesses and helped fund many projects, such as the Sassoon Docks. Later in life he moved to England, where he lived in grand houses in London and Brighton. He was given a baronetcy in 1890 and died here in 1896 at the age of 78, indeed finding his resting place in his purpose-built oriental mausoleum on the Sussex coast. In 1912 his son Edward was also buried here.

By 1933, their remains were transferred to the Willesden Jewish Cemetery in London and the building sold. Since then it has been through many uses, including serving as an air raid shelter. In 1949 it was bought by the Kemp Town Brewery Company and annexed to the Hanbury Arms pub next door. While the outside remained largely unchanged, the interior was furnished in an oriental manner, with murals depicting dancing girls and elephants. For many years it was known as the Bombay Bar and it now houses the Proud Cabaret Brighton club. The murals are long gone, but the interior and ambience are still lush and exotic.

Address Proud Cabaret Brighton, 83 St Georges Road, BN2 1EF, +44 (0)1273 605789, www.proudcabaretbrighton.com, brightonreservations@proud.co.uk | Getting there 15-minute walk from the Royal Pavilion; bus 12, 12A, 12X ,13X, 14, 27 to Paston Place, or 37, 37B to Abbey Road | Hours Please check Proud Cabaret Brighton's website for performance listings and timings. The venue can be hired for private events. | Tip If you want to see where Albert Sassoon lived in Brighton just walk down Paston Place until you reach the magnificent grade II-listed Eastern Terrace. Sassoon owned the circular no. 1, where he entertained high society and even royalty. In 1999 the terrace was used in a film adaptation of Graham Greene's novel The End of the Affair, starring Ralph Fiennes and Julianne Moore.

74_ Shoreham Airport
A Modernist haven for plane spotters

The greater Brighton area has outstanding examples of Modernist architecture, including the recently reopened Lido at Saltdean, Embassy Court near Hove (see ch. 23) and the Furze Hill complex by St Ann's Well Gardens (see ch. 77). The most exciting larger structure is this, the oldest working commercial airport in the country. Its terminal building and hangar date from the 1930s, but the flying fields were used as early as 1910, when local aviator Harold Piffard took off in his hand-built biplane, 'Hummingbird'. Commercial cargo flights soon followed, and the airport played an important role during World War I.

In 1930, it was purchased jointly by Brighton, Hove and Worthing, with the aim to establish a substantial municipal airport. The distinctive Modernist buildings were created to designs by R. Stavers Hessell Tiltman and it opened officially as Brighton Hove and Worthing Joint Municipal Airport in 1936. It was a strategic airport in World War II and, being in prime location on the south coast, was targeted by German bombers. Damaged only slightly, the buildings survive largely intact and unaltered and are often used in movies and documentaries.

Passenger flights resumed after the war and its official name is now Brighton City Airport. Not as substantial as Gatwick Airport, it has four runways and six helipads, and deals with around 50,000 flights per year. The airport welcomes visitors, even those with no intention of taking off. You can watch landings and take-offs on the longest runway on a live webcam or marvel at the Art Deco interiors in the Hummingbird Café, which serves great traditional breakfasts, lunches and cake. There is a small museum, and guided tours can be booked. Events great and small take place at the airport all year round. If there is nothing special on, it is the most peaceful place for a cup of coffee and a dream.

Address The Terminal Building, Cecil Pashley Way, BN43 5FF, +44 (0)1273 467373, flybrighton.com, reception@flybrighton.com | **Getting there** By car follow signs to the airport from A27; 18-minute walk from Shoreham-by-Sea Railway Station; bus 700 Coastliner to Adur Recreation Ground, then 10-minute walk | **Hours** Mon–Fri 8am–8pm, Sat 9am–8pm, Sun 9am–7pm; café Mon–Sat 7am–6pm, Sun 7am–5pm | **Tip** From the airport you get a great view of the chapel of Lancing College, an independent boarding and day school founded in 1848. The Gothic Revival chapel dominates the skyline north-west of the airfields and is one of the tallest vaulted churches in the country.

75 — Shoreham Port Locks
Watch the ships go by

Shoreham Port (often misnamed Shoreham Harbour, which is only part of it) is a busy port with a lot of history. It stretches from Hove Lagoon through Portslade, Southwick and Shoreham (see ch. 44). Its ship canal branches off from the estuary of the River Adur, running parallel with the shoreline, and is nearly three kilometres long. Cycle, walk or jog from Brighton centre to this lesser-known and quieter area of Greater Brighton, or hop on the 700 Coastliner bus and you can admire a fully working commercial port close-up. If you have an appetite for ship-spotting and industrial marine architecture and technology, then this is the place to come.

The first lock was built on the site of the present dry dock in 1850, and a few years later the canal was opened for shipping. Gas works were constructed on the south bank in 1870, and by the end of the century the Corporation of Brighton built an electric power station. The port was thriving in the early 20th century, and by the 1930s the canal had been deepened to allow larger ships to enter. A new lock was opened by Prince George, Duke of Kent, in 1933. The original power station doesn't exist anymore, but a new one, which proudly dominates the skyline, was built in 2000. Shoreham Port has recently made an effort to reduce its dependency on fossil fuels and in 2016, shortly after its 250th anniversary, erected two wind turbines on the outer lay-by terminal. These supply the energy for the port's pump house.

A walk around the locks in the eastern harbour arm is surprisingly calming. You can enter a path by Nautilus House, the port's headquarters and visitor centre. The path crosses the canal, dry dock and lock via bridges and walkways. This public footpath is open day and night, but if a ship comes into a lock and you are on the southern side of a bridge, all you can do is wait patiently and enjoy the spectacle.

Address Shoreham Port, Nautilus House, 90–100 Albion Street, BN42 4ED, +44 (0)1273 598100, www.shoreham-port.co.uk, info@shoreham-port.co.uk | Getting there 5-minute walk from Southwick Railway Station; bus 700 Coastliner to Grange Road then 2-minute walk | Hours Always accessible | Tip When you get to the end of the footpath and reach Basin Road South on the seafront, turn left, enjoy the views of Brighton from a distance and go for some tasty food and drinks in Carats Café Bar (www.caratscafebar.com).

76__Spence's Meeting House
A concrete kaleidoscope of colour

The University of Sussex was one of the first 'new universities' founded in the 1960s. A campus university nestled in the gentle folds of the Sussex Downs approximately 6 kilometres east of Brighton, it was designed by Sir Basil Spence just after finishing his unflinchingly modern Coventry Cathedral, rebuilt from the ashes of World War II.

Here he employed a cross-shaped layout, using predominantly concrete, iron and red brick. His architectural language was one of symmetry and clarity, drawing on classical ideas as well as local building materials and traditions.

The first buildings from the early 1960s are monumental, with little ornament, yet designed with great concern for the emotional well-being of students and staff (see ch. 28).

The original plans did not include a place of worship, and the Meeting House, open to all worshippers regardless of their beliefs, was added in 1966 after a large donation from Sir Sydney Caffyn. Keeping the design simple, with no external religious symbols, Spence built a circular island of peace and calm into a glade of mature trees, surrounded by a rain-water moat, with full-length clear windows on the ground floor. The upper-floor chapel is constructed of rough concrete blocks with thin panes of coloured glass set into the recesses, topped by a conical copper roof. A roof light in the shape of an eye illuminates the altar.

The complex arrangement of colours can be interpreted in several ways, but the use of glass and light in this chapel is above all simply beautiful. Lit inside at night, the building becomes a kaleidoscopic beacon; in strong sunlight the interior is flooded in colours. If you can, visit on an autumn afternoon, when the sun is low. The powerful combination of raw concrete, fragile coloured glass and the overall simplicity of the interiors makes this building one of Spence's overlooked masterpieces.

Address University of Sussex, Falmer, BN1 9QF, www.sussex.ac.uk/chaplaincy | **Getting there** 5-minute walk from Falmer Railway Station; bus 5B, 23, 25, 25X, 28, 29, 29B, 29X, 50 to Falmer Station | **Hours** Generally open during the day. Visitors are welcome but should respect worshippers. See website for details of events and services. | **Tip** There are more architectural marvels to be found on Sussex University campus, and you can also go for a long walk on the Sussex Downs north and east of campus. To the west is Stanmer Park (see ch. 84).

77 __ St Ann's Well Gardens
An unexpected paradise in the city

There are many great parks in Brighton and Hove, but this one is extra special, and is rarely stumbled across by tourists. It is in a wholly residential area less than a kilometre inland from the beach, north of the Brunswick Town area. It can also be reached from the east if you head into one of the side streets off Montpelier Road, but you really have to look for it. Then, suddenly, a large park reveals itself, with many intriguing features, lots of wildlife, and possibly the best café any parent of playground-age children can dream of.

The park wasn't always so urban. Before the area was built up it was in relatively open land between Brighton and Hove. It gets its name from the ancient 'Chalybeate' spring located near its Furze Hill entrance. The spring's iron-rich water was a great attraction in Georgian and Victorian times, when its flow was so strong that it qualified as a spa, and a large pump house was built over it. It must have been a great addition to Brighton's attraction as the 'watering place' (see ch. 54). By the early 20th century the flow had diminished and the pump house was pulled down in the interwar years. A mock well now marks the spot.

The park flourished even without the spa. It is formed of gently sloping hills with winding paths and has a large number of native and exotic mature trees. No wonder squirrels love the place: the population here is so large, the park has been nicknamed 'squirrel park'. There are protected wildlife conservation areas, a fish pond, a rose garden, a large playground, and plenty of space for games and picnics, as well as tennis courts and a bowling green for sporty types. On a hot summer's day many locals decamp here, and it seems this park has everything one could possibly need in life.

The fully licensed Garden Café is perfectly located overlooking a large lawn, so parents can enjoy a cuppa while keeping an eye on the kids.

Address Entrances to the park in Nizells Avenue, Furze Hill and Summerhill Road, nearest postcode BN3 1NF | **Getting there** 15-minute walk from Brighton Railway Station; bus 21A to Furze Hill, or 7, 93 to Montefiore Road | **Hours** Always open; café daily 8am–4.15pm (www.thegardencafehove.co.uk) | **Tip** On its southern side the park is flanked by a very attractive range of 1930s' apartment blocks, built around the same time as Embassy Court (see ch. 23). Furze Croft and Wick Hall, both by the architect R. Toms & Partners, are super-chic examples of British 'Moderne' style.

78 St Margaret's Rottingdean
Pre-Raphaelite gems of a very personal kind

The Rottingdean parish church proudly informs visitors that it has been serving the village and its surrounding area since before the Norman Conquest. In Sussex ancient churches abound, but this one has extra treats in store.

The building is an intriguing mixture of medieval features and more recent additions, for example the 1897 'Lych-gate', where coffins were placed before a funeral. The original Saxon church here was probably considerably smaller than what greets us today, and an 11th-century bell tower is known to have collapsed soon after it was built, demolishing large parts of the church. The present 12th-century tower has massive walls, but this didn't put an end to the building's troubles. Villagers fled to the church during one of many French raids in 1377, but the French set it on fire, and everyone inside perished. It was rebuilt and extended in the following centuries. In 1856 it underwent a major restoration by the architect Sir George Gilbert Scott (see ch. 97).

At some point the church was named after St Margaret of Antioch, the patron saint of pregnancy and childbirth. A stone carving of her head graces the west entrance. The Pre-Raphaelite painter Edward Burne-Jones lived in the white-washed North End House across the green from 1880 until his death in 1898. Although there are several examples of his stained-glass work in churches in the Brighton area (see ch. 80), the seven here are particularly moving. Made by William Morris to Burne-Jones' designs, they include elegant figures of St Margaret and the Virgin in cobalt blue robes in the chancel. The windows above the altar depict the archangels Gabriel, Michael and Raphael, and were a gift from Burne-Jones to commemorate his daughter's marriage here in 1893. Two further lancet windows were installed after his and Morris' deaths. Burne-Jones' ashes lie in the churchyard, in a spot he chose, visible from North End House.

Address The Green, Rottingdean, BN2 7HA, +44 (0)1273 309216, www.stmargaret.org.uk | Getting there Bus 2, 57, 84 to Rottingdean Pond or 2, 12, 14, 27, 47 to Rottingdean White Horse | Hours Mon–Sat 10am–2pm, Sun 8am–noon. Please respect worshippers and check services and events on the website. | Tip From here it is only a 20-minute walk up to Rottingdean Windmill, silhouetted starkly against the sky in the west. You will be rewarded with spectacular views over the Sussex Downs and the sea.

79__St Mary's Church Shoreham

Acoustic and visual beauty on a large scale

Many of the ancient churches in Sussex were given a 19th-century makeover. St Mary de Haura (meaning 'at the harbour'), built around 1100 in the Norman town of New Shoreham, is an exception. For much of the Middle Ages it was one of the largest and most important parish churches in the county and has ancient links with pilgrims and crusaders who set sail to the Holy Land from Shoreham Harbour (see ch. 44 and 75). It has since lost half of its length, but has mercifully escaped any major redecoration or rebuilding, and is a stunning example of a Norman church, and deservedly grade I-listed. If it was in the centre of a large city it would be overrun with people. Set back from the main harbour area, it is an extraordinarily peaceful place, ideal for anyone with an interest in medieval architecture, flora and music.

The cruciform church with its flat-roofed tower and rounded arches is surrounded by a beautiful churchyard, where you can trace the outline of the 30-metre-long nave, demolished or collapsed sometime in the 17th century. A piece of its west wall survives and was recently cleared of ivy and stabilised.

There is also a delightful 'hortus conclusus' or enclosed medieval garden, planted in 2003 for the church's 900th anniversary. The symbolic meaning of its flowers – daisies, cowslips, lilies, peonies, snowdrops, violets and many more – would have been understood by the Christian population of medieval Shoreham. A guide to the plants is available on the website and in the church.

The acoustics in the tall vaulted chancel and aisles are so good that the building is frequently used for concerts, plays, exhibitions and other cultural events. For a magical, easy-to-organise experience you could come for choral evensong, which takes place every third Sunday of the month at 6pm.

Address Church Street, BN43 5DQ, +44 (0)1273 440202, www.stmarydehaura.org.uk, smdh.office@gmail.com | Getting there 10-minute walk from Shoreham-by-Sea Railway Station; bus 2, 3, 19, 60, 700 to Crown & Anchor | Hours Daily 9am–6pm, main Sunday service 10am | Tip This is an ideal area for strolling. Walk down Church Street or East Street towards the River Adur and you will see the Adur Ferry Bridge, a pedestrian bridge opened in 2013. It links the town centre with Shoreham Beach and is a great spot for watching sunsets.

80 St Michael & All Angels

Two stunning churches in one

This grandiose church has been called Brighton's 'cathedral of the back streets'. Serving the areas of Montpelier and Clifton Hill, it is an inclusive church in the Catholic tradition of the Church of England, which means you can expect copious amounts of frankincense at Christmas mass. It is without a doubt one of the finest examples of a highly decorated Victorian church in the South of England, bursting with magnificent stained-glass windows by the Pre-Raphaelites William Morris, Edward Burne-Jones (see ch. 78), Ford Maddox-Brown, Dante Gabriel Rossetti, Philip Webb and Peter Paul Marshall. Other beautiful features include a high altar of red Italian marble and Sussex marble pillars.

St Michael's is actually two churches, built in relatively quick succession in the later 19th century. The older part, built in 1860–61, was designed by George Frederick Bodley in an Italianate style and now forms the south aisle. It was consecrated in 1862 and had room for a 700-strong congregation. Astonishingly, not even that proved big enough for the growing population of Victorian Brighton, and plans were soon made to enlarge the church, using designs by William Burges. A second, cathedral-like church was added to the north of Bodley's church, whose north aisle was demolished in the process. Burges' church was completed in 1895 and now forms the nave. He had originally intended to include a campanile and a cloister, but these were never built.

There are too many gorgeous stained-glass windows to list here, but a highlight is Edward Burne-Jones' *Flight into Egypt*, which is at low level in the Lady Chapel in the Bodley Church. Look out, too, for the dark grey limestone steps in here, made of Derbyshire limestone. You can see fossilised remains of sea lilies in them. For those interested in the architectural history of the church, an excellent guidebook by David Beevers is available.

Address Victoria Road, BN1 3FU, +44 (0)1273 822284, saintmichaelsbrighton.com, saintmichaelbrighton@gmail.com | **Getting there** 10 minute walk from Brighton Railway Station; many buses to Churchill Square, then a 5-minute walk uphill | **Hours** Usually open during the day depending on staffing. Check website for Mass times. Main sung Mass Sun 10.30am. | **Tip** The long-running Friends of St Michael's is a membership-based organisation that contributes to the care of the building and its fixtures, fittings and artwork. They frequently put on fundraising cultural and community events, such as concerts, lectures, parties, and guided tours, which are open to the general public (saintmichaelsbrighton.com/friends-of-st-michaels).

81_ St Nicholas Rest Garden

Time to reflect, away from the crowds

Walk up Dyke Road from Churchill Square for just a few hundred metres and look out for a large stone archway to your left. Behind it you will find one of the least-known green spaces in central Brighton. St Nicholas was originally a cemetery and is now a public park, perfect for a bit of reflective wandering among the remains of Victorian gothic tombs. The long, south-facing garden is frequently drenched in sunlight. Because it is built on the slopes of the Clifton Hill area, you even get views of the sea from the upper terrace, albeit through a curtain of urban structures.

By 1840, the parish church St Nicholas of Myra had run out of burial space for the second time, and the churchyard was extended with this piece of land on the opposite side of Dyke Road from the church. It was only used for burials until 1853, by which time the much larger Extra-Mural Cemetery off Lewes Road had been created (see ch. 26). In 1940, most of the gravestones were moved to the boundary walls to create an open green space.

The layout and design of the garden was the work of the famous local architect Amon Henry Wilds (see ch. 47, 62 and 91). He created the archway as well as the 14 burial vaults at the north end, some of which still contain coffins. Only number 13 has wooden doors and is now a tool shed for the gardeners. It is possible that no coffin was ever placed in number 13 because of superstition about the number. Wilds had envisaged a huge pyramid-shaped vault with room for over a thousand coffins in his designs, but it was never built.

In various stages of beautiful decay, the terrace of vaults gives the place a sense of architectural unity and looks particularly evocative when a storm is coming in from the sea or mist is rolling in. Photographers can often be seen trying to capture the gothic character of the place. In the summer months the garden is sometimes used for concerts and open-air theatre.

Address Dyke Road, opposite St Nicholas Church, BN1 3LJ | **Getting there** 10-minute walk from Brighton Railway Station; many buses to Churchill Square | **Hours** Daily dawn – dusk | **Tip** St Nicholas Rest Garden is in the Montpelier and Clifton Hill Conservation Area, which boasts many architectural treasures. Just north of the garden is the very elegant Clifton Terrace, which has a delightful alley, Vine Place, running along its back. Both have starring roles in Nigel Richardson's amusing memoir Breakfast in Brighton: Adventures on the Edge of England.

82 St Paul's Angel Lectern
Tiers of angels will sweep you off your feet

West Street, once the western border of the medieval fishing village of Brighthelmstone, has long been the trajectory to the seafront. Many visitors tumble out of Brighton Railway Station and head straight down Queen's Road, and, following the whiff of the sea, continue south after the Clock Tower, along West Street, until they reach the beach. By day, West Street is busy with shoppers. Cars line up to enter the multi-storey car parks. By night, this is club and party land. It is in this noisy and often raucous area that you can find one of the most exquisite examples of late 19th-century sculpture – the angel lectern in St Paul's Church.

St Paul's was built in 1848 as a mission for Brighton's fishermen and their families, paid for by the Revered Henry Michell Wagner, Vicar of Brighton (see ch. 64). Designed by the architect Richard Cromwell Carpenter, it has a relatively austere exterior and a distinctive, beacon-like bell tower, but also has a complete series of stained-glass windows by Gothic Revival designer A. W. N. Pugin, which stand out in glorious colour against the simpler interior. After the church's completion, an ecclesiastical journal boasted that at last 'Brighton's hideous chapels are to be shamed by a real church'.

Over the decades, further ornamental objects were added, and the interiors are now a stunning example of the Gothic Revival style morphing into Aestheticism and the Arts and Crafts Movement. Of these later additions, the brass lectern, made in 1885 by the Birmingham firm Hardman, Powell and Co, is the dreamiest. Based on motifs from the Apocalypse, tiers of beautiful angels play trumpets, fight storms and emerge from clouds, dramatically surrounding the cylindrical gothic column. At the of top, two majestic angels hold up the actual reading desk. If these angels can't transport you away from the hustle and bustle of central Brighton, nothing will.

Address 60 West Street, BN1 2RS, +44 (0)1273 203231, www.saintpaulschurch.org.uk |
Getting there 10-minute walk from Brighton Railway Station; many buses to Churchill
Square | Hours Generally open during the day. Please respect worshippers. See website for
details of events and services. | Tip A narrow side passage leads from the church entrance in
West Street to the main church. In it you will find a rare 1916 example of a 'street shrine'.
Initially used to list the names of the men serving in World War I, the devastating death toll
quickly turned these boards into shrines, where locals left flowers and candles.

83___ St Peter's, Preston Park
Centuries of stories in one tiny church

Behind Preston Manor (see ch. 65) sits a small, square-towered church surrounded by a mossy churchyard. This serene setting and the deceptively simple appearance of St Peter's betrays its dramatic history. Sometimes confused with a larger, younger church of the same name in central Brighton, north of the Royal Pavilion, this little-known gem has a much longer history, and boasts many beautiful features.

It was built from local flint in around 1250 as the parish church of Preston, then a small village north of Brighton, on land held by the Bishop of Chichester. There may have been an earlier church on the site. Remarkably, the outer shape of the church has not changed much since the 13th century. Inside, the entire wall above and around the chancel arch was decorated with colourful frescos, depicting the nativity, St Michael weighing souls, and the murder of St Thomas Becket.

Sadly, a fire devastated the church in 1906, destroying most of the paintings, but some faint figures can still be seen. Gone, too, are the tall box pews for up to 216 paying worshippers and the free backless benches for up to 116 poorer parishioners, removed in 1872. But many interesting elements survive. The unusual altar was originally the chest tomb of Edward Elrington, who lived in the manor in the 16th century. Set into the wall to its right are three sedilia – medieval seats for priests. The recently restored chancel stencils and most stained-glass windows date from the Edwardian era, the latter made by Lavers, Barraud & Westlake. There are charming carvings on the pews, including heads of Native Americans, kings, queens, and biblical figures. The church also tells a gruesome Victorian story: a marble wall plaque commemorates Frederick Isaac Gold, murdered on a train from London in 1881. His killer was caught, following an artist's impression of his likeness, and hanged in Lewes jail.

Address Preston Park, BN1 6SD, www.stpeterprestonpark.co.uk | Getting there 10-minute walk from Preston Park Railway Station; bus 5, 5A to Preston Drove then 2-minute walk. Access is via the pathway leading from Preston Drove, or through the park, past the chalet café, and through the churchyard. | Hours Daily 10.30am–3.30pm, and often longer in summer | Tip Preston Park Tavern, a spacious, friendly gastro-pub in a residential area, is a 10-minute walk away at 88 Havelock Road (www.prestonparktavern.pub).

84 Stanmer Park
The unexpected Picturesque

It is easy to whizz past the open countryside that stretches between Brighton and Lewes, but it is worth exploring these often-overlooked areas. Stanmer Park is the largest park in Brighton and easily reached by bus – you just have to dare to get off at Stanmer Park Gates and walk a few hundred yards north. You will be rewarded with one of the best views of a landscaped country estate, nestled in the gently rolling hills of the Sussex Downs National Park, with ample opportunity for cloud-watching, picnics and woodland walks.

Stanmer Park is first mentioned in late 11th-century records and is one of few surviving historic farming estates in East Sussex. It originally comprised around 5,000 acres and included the villages of Stanmer and Falmer. It was the seat of the Pelham family (the earls of Chichester) from 1713 until 1947, when the land and house were sold to the local authority. Since then the park has been in public ownership.

It is best to enter the estate between the pretty gate houses near the bus stop. The village and house are approached via a long straight path, from where you can see the park unfolding. New views open up the closer you get to Stanmer House, with the path now gently curving in typically Picturesque manner. The surrounding park was laid out by Thomas Pelham in 1801.

Stanmer House was designed by the French architect Nicholas Dubois and built in 1722 for Henry Pelham, incorporating parts of an older building. Some of its original interior features survive and despite lacking its furnishings it is still a good example of a grand 18th-century country house. Since it was sold it has been used by several institutions, including the University of Sussex (see ch. 28 and 76). It was renovated in the early 2000s and reopened to the public in 2006. It is currently run by The House Café company, who have opened a restaurant in the library, with additional dining space in the garden (www.thehousecafe.co.uk).

Address Lewes Road, BN1 9SE, www.brighton-hove.gov.uk | **Getting there** 10-minute walk from Falmer Railway Station; bus 23, 25, 25X, 50U, 78 to Stanmer Park. Also accessible via footpaths from the South Downs and University of Sussex. | **Hours** Always accessible | **Tip** In the village of Stanmer you will find delightful traditional tea rooms, where hot food and drinks are served daily, 10am–4pm, slightly longer at weekends, all year round (apart from Christmas Day). The décor and style don't seem to have changed much since the 1950s, when they first opened (stanmertearooms.com).

85 __ Toy and Model Museum

Play with your childhood memories here

Beneath Brighton Railway Station is one of the country's most endearing museums. Step through a small door in the arches under the forecourt and you may think you have just entered Dr Who's TARDIS. The Brighton Toy and Model Museum opens up a world full of childhood dreams and memories, and is the opposite of minimalist.

The warmly lit rooms of the museum are packed with toys that generations of children – and probably quite a few adults – used to play with. This is in fact one of the finest collections of toys and models in the world, boasting over 10,000 exhibits, including examples from the world's top toy makers, and a priceless model train collection. A unique, fully working O-gauge electric railway, on which some of the trains date from before the 1930s, will probably tempt you to start building a set in your spare room.

Given the location of the museum it is fitting that the transport theme features so largely. Apart from the large collection of Hornby O-gauge trains there is also a popular 'Spot-On' display of die-cast cars made by manufacturers such as Corgi, Dinky and Budgie in the mid-20th century. One often sees excited visitors here exclaiming that that they had 'one just like that!'. The recognisability of many of these toys makes a visit to this gem of a museum so emotional. Some objects are more than 100 years old, and tell of a lost world, and how childhood has changed, such as the model Bavarian grocery shop with miniature scales, jars and tins, or rare dolls' houses complete with furniture.

There are also large-scale radio-controlled aeroplanes and helicopters, arguably the precursors of drones, as well as old-fashioned penny arcade games and a working 19th-century 'Mutoscope', displaying early photographic animation. Unleash your own inner child here, or show today's children how toys developed from tin and wood to today's electronic devices.

Address 52–55 Trafalgar Street, BN1 4EB, +44 (0)1273 749494, www.brightontoymuseum.co.uk, info@brightontoymuseum.co.uk | **Getting there** 2-minute walk from Brighton Railway Station; many buses to Brighton Station | **Hours** Tue–Fri 10am–5pm, Sat 11am–5pm | **Tip** Carry on further down Trafalgar Street after a visit to find a range of both traditional pubs and trendy new cafés.

86 __ Tram Shelter
Modern design for an old-fashioned vehicle

By 1901, at the dawn of motorised transportation, the population of Brighton had doubled in 50 years to 123,000. But the motorcar was not yet for the masses, and Brighton introduced a tramway system designed to deal with the constant influx of new citizens and visitors to the increasingly popular resort.

By 1905 an approximately 15 kilometres tram system was in place, comprising eight routes taking passengers as far away as the Race Hill, Five Ways, Tivoli Crescent North, and beyond the cemeteries on Lewes Road. At first the common terminus was Victoria Gardens, but after three years the routes were extended eastward and the southern side of Steine Gardens became the new terminus.

The fleet of 80 trams served for nearly 40 years before closing in 1939 to make way for motorcars and buses. While tram technology may have been innovative, the trams always looked old fashioned, as did the tram shelters, most of which were built from wood in a rustic style, with overhanging eaves painted in cream and brown. Even the updated and electrified 1920s' shelter retained that rural look. By the mid-1930s, the designers had developed a taste for Art Deco, and in 1936 a bigger shelter, with underground public loos, was erected on the western side of Steine Gardens. This was sleek and streamlined, with rounded corners and a flat roof, a bit like an ocean liner, and sparkled in white from the mica particles in the artificial Brizolet rendering. It was refreshingly curvaceous and modern, with a name to match: the 'Moderne' shelter.

Most of the Brighton tram shelters have disappeared (for an exception see ch. 92 Tip), with a few ending up in transport museums, but the 'Moderne' on the Steine survives and is now a café. The similar bus shelters further north, opposite the Royal Pavilion, were built in 1950, clearly inspired by their nearby predecessor. All are frequently incorrectly dated 1926.

Address Old Steine Gardens, Old Steine, Brighton, BN1 1GY | **Getting there** 15-minute walk from Brighton Railway Station; many buses to Old Steine or North Street | **Hours** Old Steine Café: daily 7.30am – 8pm | **Tip** Take a few steps north, cross St James's Street and pause at the Brighton War Memorial on the Old Steine, designed in the style of a Roman water garden and unveiled in 1922. It is inscribed with the names of 2,600 Brighton men and women who died in World War I.

87___Undercliff Walk

Bring sunglasses and raincoat, just in case

Since being by the sea is one of the main attractions of Brighton, one should make the most of it. There is much more than just the stretch of beach between the piers. If you enjoy a bit of exercise, or just a leisurely stroll, there is the Undercliff Walk, a path that runs from the Marina (see ch. 52) to the eastern Brighton & Hove City boundary at Saltdean.

The five-kilometre walk is part of Brighton coast defences, a concrete sea wall that protects the famous white chalk and flint cliffs from erosion, as it stops waves from crashing onto them. This makes the walks suitable for pedestrians, cyclists, people with buggies, toddlers with scooters, inline skaters and wheelchair users. You will be moving along the bottom of those impressive tall cliffs, which extend all the way to Newhaven, and have been identified as a Site of Special Scientific Interest in East Sussex.

Try and spot interesting geological strata and perhaps fossils in the cliffs, or just enjoy the sea views. But beware, you will be walking along a south-facing coastline, and those white cliffs reflect every bit of sunlight. You may end up with an unexpected sunburn, and in summer you must be careful of the exposure. Apply sunscreen and take water with you.

Waves sometimes crash over the wall and occasionally the path is flooded, but mostly this is a splendid area for wave-watching. At Rottingdean the beach is great for rock-pooling, and nearby shops sell nets and buckets. The Undercliff Walk is dotted with cafés and refreshment stalls, and there is nothing better than sipping a cup of hot tea on a winter walk along here. Erosion remains a problem, despite much work that has been carried out to protect and stabilise the soft and brittle cliffs. Occasionally, especially after heavy rain, the cliffs become unstable and have to be closed because of likely rock falls.

Address Rottingdean, BN2 7AZ, www.brighton-hove.gov.uk | **Getting there** Bus 7 to and from the Marina; buses 12, 12A, 14, 14C, 27, 27C run along the seafront towards Seaford, Eastbourne, Newhaven or Saltdean and back; free parking available at the Marina, paid parking at other starting points | **Hours** Always open, apart from temporary closures due to cliff fall | **Tip** If you haven't had enough spectacular scenery, hop on the No. 12 Coaster anywhere along the Undercliff Walk. Hailed as 'one of the most scenic bus routes in England' it takes you all the way to Beachy Head in Eastbourne, and many other beautiful spots along the coast, in less than an hour.

88 Unicorn Bookshop House
A historic hippie site

On the edge of the North Laine stands a corner house that was once the site of the notorious Unicorn Bookshop, run from 1965 to 1975 by the openly gay American poet and occultist William Huxford Butler, known as Bill Butler. He specialised in modern poetry, and stocked literature by writers such as Alan Ginsberg, Henry Miller and J. G. Ballard, considered by some to be incendiary and obscene.

While very much associated with hippie culture, there was nothing mild-mannered or flowery about The Unicorn Bookshop. Butler also published pamphlets under the name Unicorn Press and helped others produce small publications on his printing press. The shop became a haven for philosophical and political debate. Many famous writers visited, such as Graham Greene, who called it 'one of the most interesting bookshops in Great Britain'. Butler commissioned John Upton, one of the UK's first street artists, to paint psychedelic motifs, including a unicorn, on the outside of the house. It was painted over after the bookshop closed.

Butler paid a high price for pushing boundaries: in 1968 an obscenity lawsuit was brought against him for having published a pamphlet by J. G. Ballard, *Why I Want to Fuck Ronald Reagan*. He was fined, and appealed, but ultimately lost a lot of money. Despite support from friends and allies he went bankrupt and relocated to rural Wales, where he died of a drug overdose in 1977.

In 2017, sponsored by Brighton and Hove Council and produced by Kriya Arts, Brighton street artist Sinna One (see ch. 46) painted an homage to the Unicorn Bookshop onto the building. In 2021, when The Botanist Coffee Co. opened a café in the building, this was replaced by another beautiful mural by Brighton design studio See Creatures, which still makes visual references to this exciting part of Brighton's history of counterculture.

THE BOTANIST COFFEE CO.

FREDERICK STREET

see creatures

50 A

THE BOTANIST COFFEE CO.

Address 50 Gloucester Road, BN1 4AQ | Getting there 5-minute walk from Brighton Railway Station; nearest bus stop Brighton Station | Hours Always viewable | Tip If you are keen to see a real John Upton, his large 1976 mural, Christ's Entry into Brighton, hangs in a seminar room at Sussex University (see ch. 28 and 76). Ask in the School Office in the Arts A building whether it is possible to see room Arts A 155.

89 West Blatchington Mill

In full sail and worthy of a prestigious award

Brighton and its surrounding areas were once dotted with dozens of windmills, which could often be seen for miles. They served local farms, producing both flour and animal food. Many ceased operating in the later 19th century, and by the mid-20th century most had been demolished. Some leave a ghostly trace in street or house names where they once stood. Yet, some survive, and this one is a particularly lovely example – so lovely that the famous Romantic painter John Constable painted it on one of his walks in November 1825 (see ch. 42). It is well worth an excursion to the outskirts of the city.

West Blatchington Windmill dates from c.1820 and is, like many other Sussex windmills, a so-called smock-mill, in reference to the shape of the tall sloping 6- or 8-sided tower. Only the cap of the mill rotates, to face the wind, while the main body remains static. This mill's tower is a fine 6-side flint and brick structure, its upper part weather-boarded. Originally it stood in open countryside with long barns abutting three sides, but the decline of mills and urban expansion took their toll. Milling ceased in 1897, and fire destroyed its south barn in 1936. Perhaps this fire was not entirely accidental, as the roads that surround it today were laid out in the 1930s. The still picturesque mill now sits isolated but defiant on a traffic island – a reminder of Brighton and Hove's rural past. It is still very much part of local social life: at general elections it is used as a polling station.

The windmill opened to the public in 1979 and since then many volunteers and organisations have helped protect it. After a recent 74-week-long restoration project, led by the City Council, it is now fully restored and the surviving west barn has become an exhibition space. Deservedly, in 2017 the project received the prestigious Public and Community Award from the Sussex Heritage Trust.

Address Holmes Avenue, BN3 7LE, +44 (0)1273 776017, www.visitbrighton.com/things-to-do/west-blatchington-windmill-p69253 | **Getting there** 20-minute walk from Aldrington Railway Station; bus 5b, 55, 56E to St Peter's Church | **Hours** May–Sept Sun & bank holiday 2.30–5pm | **Tip** Just a few steps north of the mill is the pretty Parish Church of St Peter. Now largely a 19th- and 20th-century building, it may have Saxon or Norman origins and was possibly first built with fragments of a Roman settlement on the site.

90_ West Pier Ruin

Where starlings come to dance at dusk

Brighton has a brash and sparkly party pier, but look west and you can see the remains of another pier, slowly rusting and disappearing, already detached from the mainland. Not much of its original beauty is now visible, but it has acquired an entirely different kind of atrophied, melancholic beauty. Despite its fragile state and now shadowy contours, it is one of Brighton's most-loved structures and is cared for by the West Pier Trust.

The West Pier opened in 1866, 43 years after the Chain Pier, Brighton's first pier, of which almost no trace is left. Designed by Eugenius Birch, it began life as a promenade pier, then was extended many times, turning into a full-blown pleasure pier with theatre, concert hall, restaurant and funfair. By the 1980s it had fallen into disrepair, closed down and, despite strenuous efforts, could not be saved. Severe storms and fires in the early noughties rang the death knell for this prettiest of piers.

Eventually, the area on the beach near the lost pier was regenerated and some remains of the structure were reused. Some pieces were sold at auctions, others are on display in the nearby Fishing Museum (see ch. 12). Recently a new piazza was created just east of the i360 (see ch. 14). In this flexible public space, 24 of the West Pier's cast-iron columns were installed in a Fibonacci spiral, a pattern which is found in nature and represents balance and harmony. This 'Golden Spiral' is lit up at dusk. There are plans to rebuild one of the original kiosks and place it on the beach.

The West Pier skeleton is also one of the few urban spots left in the UK where starlings gather in their thousands and create murmurations – swirling, swooping, synchronised ballets in the air. The mesmerising spectacles usually happen at dusk in the colder autumn and winter months. Because Brighton beach faces south, they can often be seen against spectacular sunsets.

Address Brighton West Pier Trust, Kings Road, BN1 2FL, +44 (0)1273 321499, www.westpier.co.uk, info@westpier.co.uk | Getting there 20-minute walk from Brighton Railway Station; many buses to Waitrose in Western Road | Tip Some of the arches under Kingsway have been transformed into interesting independent shops. The West Pier Trust has a drop-in point in one of the spaces, The West Pier Centre, where you can learn more about its history and future.

91__ Western Pavilion

Can't have the Royal Pavilion? Build your own!

In terms of visual impact on Brighton, John Nash, who orientalised the Royal Pavilion (see ch. 22) for the Prince Regent from 1815 onwards, is the most important architect in Brighton's history. His fanciful minarets, tent-shaped roofs and onion domes have become a symbol of Brighton's daring, colourful and irreverent spirit. But there are other architects who shaped the look of Brighton in its Georgian and early-Victorian heyday, most prominently Decimus Burton, Charles Busby, Amon Wilds and his son, Amon Henry Wilds. Together they created the grandest buildings of Brighton and Hove, all of them classical and elegant (see ch. 47, 62 and 81), but none of them as daringly playful and exotic as Nash's Royal Pavilion.

None of them? There is a curious house that makes you wonder whether the Pavilion grew some underground shoots and sprouted halfway between Brighton and Hove. Look down a little cul-de-sac Western Terrace opposite Waitrose in Western Road and you see on the left a building that bears an uncanny resemblance to the Royal Pavilion. It is a gleaming, white, two-storey house that sports a large onion dome, pilasters with minaret finials, cusped arches and other oriental features. It is no surprise that you may overlook it: its north façade, which faces the Western Road shopping area, was re-fronted in the 1950s, disguising the oriental style.

This is the Western Pavilion, which the younger Wilds built for himself in 1831, a few years after he had set up his own company. Nash had finalised the complete oriental makeover of the Royal Pavilion in 1823, and the shiny new Indian-inspired royal palace clearly made a strong impression on Wilds, so much so that he unashamedly and with a good dose of humour copied some of its most exotic elements for his new house. He lived here until his death in 1857.

In the 20th century, it housed offices and is now a private house again.

Address 9 Western Terrace, BN1 2LD | Getting there 20-minute walk from Brighton
Railway Station; many buses to Waitrose in Western Road | Hours Not open to the public,
but Western Terrace is accessible | Tip The Western Pavilion is not the only unusual
building in this area. Just opposite, with its main façade on Western Road, is the fascinating
Gothic House, complete with a buttressed tower, spires and gothic arches. It was the first
building in this street, built between 1822 and 1825 by Wilds and Charles Busby. Constable
painted it when he lived in nearby Sillwood Road (see ch. 42).

92__WW2 Air-raid Shelter
A hidden warren of concrete tunnels

The children of Downs Junior School in the leafy Fiveways area of Brighton spend their break-times in generously sized playgrounds. In 1985, a workman carrying out maintenance work lifted an iron cover in one of them and soon realised that he had found an emergency exit from a large underground air-raid shelter that had been lying forgotten for more than 30 years. It turned out that this was the largest one of three shelters, then known as 'trenches', constructed from pre-cast concrete panels under the school playgrounds in 1939.

Lying three metres below the ground, the structure of narrow corridors and rooms, shaped like the number 8, was essentially untouched and intact. It offered space for up to 300 children, who would have had to sit on narrow benches along the walls of the cold and damp corridors. There is a tiny kitchen where basic meals and drinks could be prepared and a few small rooms with beds. A space little bigger than a cupboard served as a lavatory, with two wooden doors, behind which large tin buckets were placed.

In the 1990s, history teacher Diane Knapp gathered archive material and moving personal accounts from former pupils who had been in the shelters during bombing raids. These were published as a book in 1994.

In 2012, the school decided to make this historically important space accessible to school groups and eventually to the public. As part of the project, Knapp's book was re-published. The shelter first opened in 2016, with immersive sound installations, historic images and quotes along the walls, and recreations of some of the rooms, fitted with original 1940s' objects. You enter through a narrow hatch and descend a steep fixed staircase, but plans are underway to make access easier. The shelter is run entirely by volunteers, and they are doing a splendid job bringing history to life.

Address Downs Junior School, Rugby Road, BN1 6ED, takeshelter.org.uk | Getting there 10-minute walk from London Road Railway Station; bus 26, 46, 50, 79, 94, 94A to Rugby Road | Hours Regular bookable tours for the general public take place during the Brighton Fringe Festival in May, but private tours can be arranged on request. It is best to get in touch with the organisers via the contact form on the website. | Tip Opposite the eastern side of the school, outside 176 Ditchling Road, is one of the very few surviving timbered tram shelters of Brighton, dating from the early 20th century (see ch. 86).

93 Anne of Cleves' House
A Tudor marriage settlement and more

Southover High Street, originally part of a medieval southern sub-urb of Lewes, runs parallel to the main road through town, but at a lower level. A stroll along this less-trodden road is well worth it, as it is lined with architectural gems and curiosities, including the remains of the gatehouse of the Priory, the elegant Priory Crescent, parts of a 14th-century hospital, and a house once lived in by Rolling Stones drummer Charlie Watts.

There are many half-timbered houses in the street, some hidden behind later façades, but this one has very special historic significance. The two-storey timber-framed house was given by King Henry VIII to his fourth wife, Anne, as part of their divorce settlement. Anne never lived in it, but it was considered a valuable house in Tudor times. The stone incorporated in the façade was a sign of wealth and status. The earliest part, a cellar under the main hall, possibly dates from the late 13th century, while the main part was built in the late 15th century. Little changed after around 1700, with its 15th-cen-tury layout intact, it is today one of the most important examples of a medieval Wealden dwelling.

The house was given to the Sussex Archaeological Society in 1923, which restored it and opened it to the public. The delightful garden sports Tudor planting schemes with traditional plants, including a medlar tree. Inside, the parlour, bedchambers, kitchen and hall give visitors a sense of an entirely different way of living. There is plenty of period furniture, including a four-poster bed, allowing you to explore how Tudors and Elizabethans lived, worked and relaxed at home. One gallery tells the story of the Sussex Wealden iron industry. There are few historic buildings that bring to life our past so beautifully.

The café and tea garden is open to both visitors and non-visitors to the museum and serves hot and cold drinks, lunches, cream teas and Tudor-inspired dishes.

Address 52 Southover High Street, BN7 1JA, +44 (0)1273 486290, sussexpast.co.uk/attraction/anne-of-cleves-house | Getting there 12-minute walk from Lewes Railway Station; local buses to Lewes High Street | Hours Tue–Sun 10am–5pm | Tip Drop in to Trinity Church on the other side of the Southover High Street and try and find the tombstone slab of Gundrada, wife of William de Warenne, founders of the Lewes Priory. She died in childbirth in 1085 and was buried in the chapter house of Lewes Priory. Their tombs were found when the railway line was dug out in 1845, and transferred to the church in 1847.

94 Bartholomew House
Shimmer and shine, strictly mathematical

The Barbican of Lewes Castle and its Keep (see ch. 95) are impressive, but when you approach them, look left to see a much later gem. Bartholomew House, a Georgian domestic building, stands at an odd angle to the Barbican forecourt, directly bordering the Castle Keep. Lewes boasts many elegant Georgian town houses, but this one is particularly intriguing and, in certain lights, glows.

Bartholomew House dates from c.1814. Possibly built by the famous local architect Amon Wilds (see ch. 26, 47, 81, 91 and 102 Tip), it is in many ways typically late-Georgian: tall, symmetrical, with white sash windows, a shallow roof and elegant panelled doors under fanlights. However, it has some strange and unfathomable features. While narrow, it has two front doors and an oddly proportioned central sash window. But what really stands out is its shimmering black façade, which turns to gold in late afternoon sun.

The façade may look high quality, but Bartholomew House is a bit of a pretender there, being faced instead with 'mathematical tiles', which are almost exclusively found in Kent and Sussex. The earliest examples date from the 17th century but 'm-tiles' were most popular in the late 18th and early 19th century. Overlapping lipped tiles with two holes at the top for hanging on a wooden framework, they may sound complicated, but they were cheaper than the salt-glaze bricks they were imitating and useful as an extra layer of protection against the elements. With m-tiles you could effectively modernise a house, giving a medieval timber-framed building a sleek Georgian look, as was often done in Lewes. Between 1785 and 1850 it was also a way of avoiding King George III's 'brick tax'.

M-tiles are commonly black, red, yellow or cream, and are usually glazed. They are not always easy to spot, but the shimmer of the glaze can give them away, as can corners or areas of small damage, where their thinness is visible.

Address Castle Gate, BN7 1YS | Getting there 10-minute walk from Lewes Railway Station; bus 28, 29, 29B to Lewes High Street | Hours Not open to the public | Tip If you want to go on a mathematical tiles hunt in Lewes, simply walk around the castle or westward along the High Street. Among many others, there are Castle Hill House and Castle Precincts House nearby with red m-tiles, and the fittingly named Black Tile Cottage sits opposite St Anne's Church. See also ch. 70.

95 Best View of the Castle
Lewes' best side?

Lewes is an undeniably photogenic town that looks pretty from many different viewpoints. It helps that it has such a picturesque focal point: the ruin of an 11th-century castle, located prominently at the centre and the highest point in town. You can see the man-made mound of the castle, framed by old trees growing in the motte, silhouetted against the sky, from many parts of town, and sometimes it sneaks into view quite unexpectedly.

Lewes Castle is one of many defensive structures built in the immediate aftermath of the Battle of Hastings and the Norman invasion in 1066. It was built by the Norman William de Warenne, who was a close ally to William the Conqueror and was responsible for administration of the 'Rape of Lewes' – not an assault, but one of subdivisions of medieval Sussex. Warenne and his wife Gundrada (see ch. 93 Tip) also founded the Cluniac priory at Southover (see ch. 103).

The castle was both a defensive structure and residence of William de Warenne and his wife. The location is strategic, as the River Ouse was navigable and needed to be protected. Unusually for a 'motte-and-bailey' castle, it has two mounds, Castle Mount and Brack Mount. The castle was further developed and extended throughout the Middle Ages, and in the 14th century an impressive two-gated barbican was added. Since 1922 it has been owned and run by the Sussex Archaeological Society, which operates under the name Sussex Past.

So where to go for the best view? Stroll along The Avenue and enter The Paddock, one half of the green lung of Lewes. It is a peaceful place (unless there is some community event going on), from which you not only get a splendid view of the north-eastern side of the castle, but also the patchwork pattern of private houses at the foot of the mound. This is particularly so at dusk, when the lights begin to come on in the houses.

Address 169 High Street, BN7 1YE, +44 (0)1273 486290, sussexpast.co.uk/attraction/lewes-castle | Getting there 8-minute walk from Lewes Railway Station; bus 28, 29, 29B to Lewes High Street | Hours Daily, Nov–Feb 10am–4pm, Mar–Oct 10am–5.30pm. Sun, Mon & bank holidays, opening at 11am | Tip The ticket desk is in Barbican House, which also houses the Museum of Sussex Archaeology, with local collections from the Stone Age to medieval times. Combined tickets with Anne of Cleves' House (see ch. 93) are available.

96__Bull House
Satyrs and revolutionary spirits

Lewes has no shortage of attractive houses with an interesting history, but Bull House has more history than many. The medieval, timber-framed, jettied High Street building was built as an inn just inside the 12th-century town walls. In 1583 the house was bought by Sir Henry Goring, who demolished the rear, replacing it with a brick and flint extension, but it remained an inn. The medieval front was kept, and it is likely that it was this new owner who added a number of the carved wooden satyrs crouched here and there. They may have adorned the entrance to the inn, which was notorious for brawls and even the site of a fatal stabbing in 1594.

In the 17th century the Bull Inn changed ownership again and more brawls ensued. At the end of the 17th century the house was purchased by the Reverend Thomas Barnard and the south part was converted into Westgate Chapel, which still abuts Bull House. By the mid-18th century the house was owned by the tobacconist Samuel Ollive, whose daughter married its most famous inhabitant, the revolutionary writer, philosopher and political activist Thomas Paine.

Paine lived here between 1768 and 1774, frequently holding political gatherings in the White Hart Inn further up the road, where a plaque proudly claims it as the 'cradle of American independence'. In 1774 he separated from his wife and emigrated to the British American colonies and is often considered the intellectual inspiration behind the American Revolution. In the 1790s he became involved with the French Revolution and wrote his most famous work, *Rights of Man*, in its wake. He died in America in 1809. When Lewes introduced its own legal currency, the Lewes pound, in 2008, Paine's portrait was chosen for the design on the bank notes.

Bull House is now the headquarters of the Sussex Archaeological Society, the oldest such society in England (see ch. 93 and 95).

Address 92 High Street, BN7 1XH, +44 (0)1273 486260, sussexpast.co.uk/bull-house |
Getting there 15-minute walk from Lewes Railway Station; bus 28, 29, 29B to Lewes
High Street, then 5-minute walk | Hours Not generally open to the public, but tours can be
booked at the weekend with local historic tour guide Mary Burke, +44 (0)1273 475885. See
website for details. | Tip A terracotta sculpture of Thomas Paine by artist Marcus Cornish
was installed outside Lewes Library in 2010.

97 Fitzroy House

The architectural legacy of a Victorian love story

You may think Fitzroy House is in a busy location, overlooking a pedestrianised precinct near Cliffe Bridge in the centre of town, but it used to be even busier. Before 1969, a railway viaduct ran right past its eastern side, and until the A 27 bypass was built, most east-west car traffic ran past its northern side.

This splendid example of Victorian Gothic architecture was built as a memorial library to long-standing Lewes MP Sir Henry Fitzroy in 1862. It was a gift to the people of Lewes from his loving wife, Hannah (of the wealthy Rothschild family). As an architect she chose the famous George Gilbert Scott (see ch. 78), who had just created the Albert Memorial in Kensington Gardens in London – a memorial to Queen Victoria's husband, Albert, who, like Fitzroy, had died relatively young and unexpectedly.

Scott put much emphasis on high-quality materials. The house sports lancet windows and a tall slim clocktower with a spire that pierces the sky proudly and romantically. Inside, an entrance hall with a turquoise ceiling greets you. A stone staircase with a wrought-iron balustrade and mahogany banisters leads to the upper floor. Before its relocation, the main library was in a large, top-lit octagonal room to the south of the main building, with fitted bookcases lining the walls.

The library became public property in 1897 and remained popular during the first half of the 20th century. After World War II it was moved to Albion Street, and the ornate Victorian Gothic style became deeply unfashionable. Fitzroy House fell into disrepair and only narrowly escaped demolition. The remarkable Franks family bought it in 1976 and restored it with great dedication. It was recently bought by Alison Grant, who is passionate about the house. She is in the process of carrying out major restoration and conservation work and regularly opens the house for cultural events and art exhibitions.

Address 10 High Street, BN7 2AD, +44 (0)7557 340911, www.fitzroyhouselewes.com, fitzroyhouselewes@gmail.com | **Getting there** 10 minute walk from Lewes Railway Station; bus 28, 29, 29B, 29X to Lewes Bus Station or Lewes Waitrose | **Hours** Occasionally open to the public on Heritage Open Days and for special events. For details check the websites. | **Tip** Walk up Friars Walk. After around 100 metres you will see to your right the remains of Turkish Baths, built around the same time as Fitzroy House, and a project Hannah Rothschild was initially interested in supporting. The baths closed in 1882 and fell into disrepair, but are now restored and house The Unity Centre, a spa, studio, yoga, and community space.

98_Jill's Pond

High on the Downs: from battlefield to dew ponds

The chalk piercing the folds of the South Downs above Lewes gives the countryside the lovely textured look captured so well by artists like Eric Ravilious and John Piper. You have several options for enjoying the best vantage point. For a great view of Lewes and its many hidden gardens and backyards, climb up to Lewes Castle on a clear day. To see the sun light up the Ouse Valley, the best view is from the golf club at the top of Chapel Hill, east of town. For panoramic views over the Downs, the meandering Ouse and the sea beyond, and a chance to walk on ground steeped in British history, head north-west to Landport Bottom, arguably the most serene spot in Lewes.

Part of the South Downs Area of Outstanding Natural Beauty, Landport Bottom was agricultural land for many years but has now reverted to chalk grassland, a rich but threatened wildlife habitat. At the top of the ridge is Jill's Pond, a dew pond created by a Lewes resident around the millennium, in memory of his late wife, Jill Percival. Traditionally watering places for sheep on the Downs, this dew pond was created as a place for contemplation and a haven for wildlife, and is a popular destination for walkers.

Sit quietly and you may see yellowhammers, skylarks, blue butterflies and pipits emerging from the grass. Look out for orchids, too, and the odd grass snake or adder basking in the sun.

The peace here is in stark contrast to the place's violent history, as Landport Bottom is also the site of the Battle of Lewes, fought on 14 May, 1264 between the rebel barons led by Simon de Montfort, Earl of Leicester, and the army of King Henry III. While the royalists outnumbered the rebels and were in a better strategic position, the barons won the battle and de Montfort briefly became the 'uncrowned King of England'. It is thought that many of the dead were buried in mass graves near Lewes Prison crossroads.

Address Landport Bottom, nearest postcode BN7 1QF, grid ref. TQ 3968 1115 | Getting there 15-minute walk on footpaths from the area west of Nevill Road, for example Spital Road, The Gallops or Firle Crescent; bus 28, 29, 29B to Lewes Prison | Tip For longer walks (up to 2 hours) start at Spital Road and continue northward, past the Old Racecourse to nearby Mount Harry and Black Cap or the village of Offham. When approaching Mount Harry you can see Brighton's i360 tower (see ch. 14) in the distance on a clear day.

99__Keere Street
Could this be the prettiest street in England?

Pre-20th-century Lewes was essentially a long High Street meandering from east to west, with smaller streets and alleyways going off it on either side. The little streets on the south side of the High Street towards Southover and the Grange offer beautiful glimpses of the fold of the Sussex Downs. The prettiest of these, and an ever-popular photo motif for visitors, is Keere Street, once on the western edge of the town.

Keere Street, which is first recorded in a deed from 1272, is steeped in history and stories, as well as offering a magnificent view of Priory Crescent and the hills beyond. It winds in a gentle curve down from where once stood the 14th-century West Gate of the town, until it was demolished in 1777. Look up left when you wander down and you'll see the former town wall soaring up from behind the houses, forming the eastern perimeter of some gardens. Walk with caution, though: although there is no through-traffic you still need to watch where you are going, as the steep street is part-cobbled. Legend has it that in 1799 the young George IV, when Prince of Wales (see ch. 37), drove a coach with four horses down it at breakneck speed.

Many interesting buildings line the narrow street, some hundreds of years old, but a few 20th-century infills blend in almost unnoticed. The house at the top western corner (no. 99–100 High Street) is a particularly picturesque timber-framed 16th-century house that has been an antiquarian bookshop for years. Above eye-level on the High Street side a milestone is set into it, marking the distances to Brighthelmstone (an old name for Brighton) and London. Halfway down on the left is the site of almshouses bequeathed in 1688 by the Presbyterian woollen draper, Thomas Matthew. They were closed in 1960. Further down is a plaque commemorating the children's writer and illustrator Eve Garnett, who lived at no. 12 from 1960 to 1988.

KEERE STREET
NO THROUGH ROAD
Although recorded in history that George IV,
when Prince Regent, drove a coach and four
down Keere Street for a wager, access by
vehicles to and from the High Street is now
forbidden.

BY ORDER
LEWES DISTRICT COUNCIL

Address BN7 1TY | Getting there 10-minute walk from Lewes Railway Station; bus 28, 29, 29B to Lewes High Street | Tip At the top of Keere Street, cross the main road and look for the figure of a White Lion mounted on the wall by a small car park in Westgate Street. It is a replica of the sign of the White Lion Inn that stood here until the whole row of small houses was demolished in 1936 under a slum clearance scheme. The original copper lion was saved and is now in the Town Hall.

100 Kingston near Lewes
A village nestled in the folds of the Downs

There are many pretty villages in East Sussex, but Kingston is very special indeed, and much less known among tourists, who tend to flock to nearby Rodmell, Berwick or Alfriston. Kingston appears quiet, as if slumbering in the safe arms of the Sussex Downs, despite its proximity to Lewes and some 20th-century housing developments nearby. It is popular with cyclists and hikers, as it is practically on the South Downs Way, and – crucially – it has a fabulous pub, The Jugg, with a terrace where local robins watch you eat great food, hoping for crumbs.

The village is ancient and mentioned in the 11th-century Domesday Book. Walk down The Street, and you get a good impression of a typical Downland village with flint walls, a range of 18th and 19th-century houses, barns and farm buildings, some considerably older. Look out for local honey and other produce offered by some Kingston residents, but make sure you bring small change for the honesty boxes. Parts of Kingston Manor date from the 16th century and were built with stones from the destroyed Lewes Priory (see ch. 103).

The 13th-century St Pancras Church at the western end of The Street has an unusual Tapsel gate, which swings around a central pivot. Inside you may be surprised by some colourful 20th-century stained-glass windows, greatly contrasting in style: one depicts a bucolic rural scene (designed in 1983 by Michael Charles Farrar Bell), another one offers a powerful abstract design by Irish artist Maud Cotter (1992).

Kingston is surrounded by simply stunning countryside: west of the church the majestic Kingston Hill rises, and if you have the energy to climb it you will be rewarded with views over miles of gently ridged, sloping chalk grassland. Walk east towards Lewes and you pass the reconstructed Ashcombe Mill, a six-sailed post mill originally built in 1828. In high summer you will serenaded by skylarks.

Address The Juggs: The Street, Kingston, Lewes, BN7 3NT, +44 (0)1273 472 523, thejuggs.co.uk | Getting there Bus 28 or 29 from Brighton, get off at Kingston Ridge, turn right into Ashcombe Hollow and walk for about a mile; by car, on the A27, take the turn for Kingston at the Ashcombe Roundabout, follow Ashcombe Hollow | Hours The Juggs: Mon, Wed–Sat noon–11pm, Sun noon–7pm; check website for food serving times | Tip Look out for a curious round domed brick building by the Ashcombe Roundabout, south of the A27. This is the surviving one of a pair of early-19th-century toll houses. It marked the beginning of the Brighton turnpike road from the east, opened in 1820 and in use until the 1870s. It provided accommodation for turnpike keepers (sussexheritagetrust.org.uk/projects-ashcombe-toll-house).

101__ The Lewes Arms

A pub as defiant as it is cosy

The Lewes Arms pub nestles at the foot of Brack Mount, the man-made motte in the shadow of Lewes Castle, just north of Castle Mount (see ch. 95). It has been there since the end of the 18th century. Judging by its location and exterior you might imagine you have stumbled upon the most tranquil of English public houses, but you'd be mistaken.

The inside is delightfully cavernous and disorientating for a first-time visitor, with a front and back bar. The front bar was for many years a no-go area for anyone who had not lived in Lewes for at least 50 years, but things are more relaxed these days. On a mild summer evening its guests spill out into the narrow medieval street in front, forcing anyone who dares to bring a car into the area to surrender.

There is a beer garden upstairs at the back, practically perching on Brack Mount, and the small function room boasts a miniature stage. The 'Armpit', as it is affectionately known, hosts many a weird and wonderful event, from full-scale pantomimes to the annual World Pea-Throwing Championships and pretend spaniel races (you don't have to bring a spaniel – any animal dressed like a spaniel will do).

In 2006, the pub became the centre of an unlikely beer revolution when then-owners Greene King brewery stopped serving the locally brewed Harvey's bitter. They had underestimated the feistiness of Lewesians, who decided to boycott their beloved pub and famously introduced 'non-loyalty' cards, stamped with every drink consumed elsewhere that could have been had at the Lewes Arms. Local politicians got involved and emotions ran high for months. The press covered the story nationally and internationally, while the pub stood nearly deserted and takings plummeted by 90 per cent. Eventually Greene King admitted defeat and started serving Harvey's again. It is fair to say that the defiant spirit of Lewes is reflected in the Lewes Arms.

Address 1 Mount Place, BN7 1YH, +44 (0)1273 473152, www.lewesarms.co.uk, lewesarms@gmail.com | **Getting there** 10-minute walk from Lewes Railway Station; bus 28, 29, 29B to Lewes High Street | **Hours** Mon–Thu 11am–11pm, Fri & Sat 11am–midnight, Sun noon–11pm | **Tip** A stone's-throw away, in Castle Ditch Lane, is the Star Brewery. No beer is brewed here, but more than 20 artists, designers and craftsmen have their studios in the 18th-century building. Many welcome visitors, and there is a small gallery space for exhibitions.

102 — Lewes Depot
A philanthropist's cinematic dream

By 1971, all three of Lewes' cinemas had disappeared, and the silver screen only existed in clubs in churches and the like. For the real cinema experience you had to venture to Brighton or Uckfield. In 2017, though, Lewes finally had its own cinema again. More ambitious and stylish than any before, it was the fruit of many years of work, investment and passion, inspired by a dream.

Run by the Lewes Community Screen charity, it was the brainchild of two film buffs, Robert Senior and Carmen Slijpen. Over several years and despite setbacks they created a community venue that is much more than just a fabulous three-screen cinema. It took its name from the depot of famous local brewery Harvey's and, before then, the General Post Office depot. Businessman and philanthropist Senior decided to make this cinema with extras his legacy and gift to Lewes, while Slijpen is the seemingly ever-present creative director. The 1930s' red-brick GPO building was incorporated into the sleek, modern venue, which combines glass, flint and metal with wood and subtle lighting. On warm days, a large outdoor space allows guests to lounge on sofas or lie on the grass while waiting for the screenings to start. The venue also houses a permanent artwork by Royal Academician Stephen Chambers: *The Big Country*, inspired by a 1958 Western by William Wyler, comprises 78 visually connected screen-prints and can be admired in the main building.

Within days of opening, Lewes Depot had become a social hub. It offers heavily reduced cinema tickets to anyone under 25, multi-purpose rooms for hire and special events, and also runs a number of courses for people as young as five. It also has a café and restaurant. One wonders how many commuters are lured in by the warm lights when they return home from London. It is just what Lewes needed, a cinema and much more – a place to be.

Address Pinwell Road, Lewes, BN7 2JS, +44 (0)1273 525354, lewesdepot.org | Getting there 1-minute walk from Lewes Railway Station; bus 28, 29, 29B to Lewes High Street | Hours Cinema: daily 10am – 11pm; café: Mon – Wed 9am – 11pm, Thu – Fri 9am – 11.30pm, Sat 10am – 11.30pm, Sun 10am – 11pm; restaurant: daily 10am – 9pm | Tip Stroll up Pinwell Road towards Friars Walk and visit All Saints, a 15th-century church, adapted in the early 19th century by Amon Wilds (see ch. 91). It closed in 1975 and is now an arts and community centre, hosting a variety of cultural events.

103 Lewes Priory Park

All the needs of medieval monks

A stone's throw from Lewes Railway Station is the peaceful Priory Park, nestled at the foot of the South Downs. It is part of a huge, medieval, monastic estate that was once home to the nearly 100 monks of the Priory of St Pancras, who came from Cluny in Burgundy after the Norman Conquest and stayed for 450 years.

The church and cloisters were largely destroyed in the 16th century during the Dissolution of the Monasteries under Henry VIII. Wandering among the remains (the refectory, the dormitories and substantial toilet blocks) evokes the domestic side of religious life, a reminder that the monks had physical as well as spiritual needs! A scale model of the original layout and excellent interpretation panels help envisage how the estate once looked. The priory ruins are now managed by the Lewes Priory Trust charity on behalf of Lewes Town Council. It aims to preserve and enhance the remains of the priory and the surrounding area and increase public awareness of its cultural and historic significance.

This priory had many gardens and orchards and some of the food eaten by the monks was grown within the priory grounds. Visit the on-site community kitchen garden to see examples of vegetables that were commonly cultivated. The quirky turreted folly tower next to the kitchen garden marks the north-west boundary of the park.

At the opposite end, close to where the infirmary once stood, is a charming herb garden where herbs used for healing, cooking, dyeing, decoration and strewing are grown. A small orchard of local Sussex apple varieties is a nod to the much larger orchard that once existed.

Look out for the monumental *The Helmet*, a 1964 sculpture by Enzo Plazzotta commemorating the Battle of Lewes of 1264 (see ch. 98). It marked the 700th anniversary of the battle, which saw the king defeated and led to the 'Mise of Lewes', a treaty restricting the authority of the monarchy.

Address Cockshut Road, Southover, BN7 1HP, www.lewespriory.org.uk, enquiries@lewespriory.org.uk | Getting there 5-minute walk from Lewes Railway Station; bus 28, 29, 29B to Lewes High Street | Hours Always open; guided tours by appointment | Tip Climb the 15-metre high ancient mount to the east of the east boundary of Priory Park. From here you get the best views over the park against the backdrop of the Downs. There are few more relaxing places to watch the sun go down.

104_Lewes Railway Land

No better place for twitchers

Lewes gives the impression of peacefulness (unless you visit in early November during the bonfire celebrations), but just a couple of minutes from the station and Cliffe High Street is a truly wild place. It is a 25-acre nature reserve on the site of former railway land at the foot of the chalk cliffs on the town's eastern edge, now managed by Lewes District Council and the Railway Land Wildlife Trust.

A network of paths takes you along the embankment of the former Lewes to Uckfield railway line, which closed in 1989, past the River Ouse that meanders through the floodplain grasslands of the reserve, and into large wooded areas full of wildlife and the remains of railway architecture. There are many large railway poplars, planted in the mid-19th century in an effort to disguise the perceived unsightliness of the railways. The reserve is a treasure trove of urban wildlife, where dog-walkers, runners, ramblers, meanderers and bird-watchers come together. This is a haven for twitchers, as the wide expanse of the grassland, lined with bushes and trees, is perfect for bird-spotting.

If you have young children you can keep them entertained for hours seeking out frogs, toads and newts in the ponds and ditches. In the densely wooded areas look out for traces in the ground of Leighside Estate, a large Victorian house that once stood here. As long as you respect the area as a nature reserve, there are very few restrictions: all footpaths are open to everyone, dogs and bicycles are allowed, and some paths are suitable for wheelchairs.

The Council and Trust have done a great job turning this land into a beautiful and educational communal space. Since 2010, the Trust operates from the Linklater Pavilion, a purpose-built sustainable structure near the Court Road entrance. It is also a centre for environmental studies and display and used for many public events.

Address Linklater Pavilion, Railway Lane, BN7 2FG, +44 (0)1273 477101, www.railwaylandproject.org | **Getting there** 5-minute walk from Lewes Railway Station. There are several entry points, but the most central one is in Court Road, with a public car park nearby. | **Hours** Always open; Linklater Pavilion open every Sun May–Sep 2–5pm, with free activity, guided walk or talk 3–4pm | **Tip** Near the Linklater Pavilion is a mound with a spiral path. This is part of a larger piece of landscape art created by Chris Drury (see ch. 30). *Heart of Reeds* is a network pattern of ditches and embankments running through the reserve, inspired by blood-flow patterns in the heart. It is best admired from the top of the adjacent chalk cliffs.

LEWES

105 The Martyrs' Prison Steps
Lewes Town Hall's dark undercroft

Lewes is a peaceful place, but every Guy Fawkes Night (5 November) it hosts the biggest, most daring bonfire celebrations in the country, celebrating the foiled 'Gunpowder Plot' to blow up Parliament in 1605. Thousands of members of bonfire societies take part, with tens of thousands of visitors arriving to watch the torch-lit processions, the huge bonfires and the fireworks. But something is different about the Lewes Bonfire Night celebrations: among the effigies of Guy Fawkes and topical political figures being lampooned in the processions (in true irreverent Lewes fashion, even effigies of the Pope have been burned), 17 burning crosses are also carried through the streets.

These are not just a reference to the Gunpowder Plot having been devised by a group of Catholics against the Protestant King James I. The Lewes Bonfire celebrations also commemorate the execution of 17 Sussex Protestant martyrs burnt at the stake here between 1555 and 1557, in the bloody reign of Queen Mary I. One of them was the Brighton brewer Deryk Carver (see ch. 9). On 22 June, 1557, ten men and women were burnt together in the largest known single burning of Protestants in British history. The executions took place outside the Star Inn on the site of what is now Lewes Town Hall, to deter others from embracing Protestantism.

The Town Hall dates from 1893, and replaced the former inn and hotel, on land owned by Lewes Priory since at least the early 14th century. Inside, a spiral staircase leads to the 14th-century barrel-vaulted undercroft where the martyrs were imprisoned before their gruesome deaths. The town council has recently revealed the external stone steps leading from the High Street down into the croft. They are covered with glass, but it is still moving to peer into this forbidding space. The commemorative plaque on the wall above sits in uneasy juxtaposition with the Town Hall noticeboard.

Address Lewes Town Hall, High Street, BN7 2QS, +44 (0)1273 471469, townhall@lewes-tc.gov.uk | **Getting there** 5-minute walk from Lewes Railway Station; bus 28, 29, 29B to Lewes High Street | **Hours** Mon–Thu 9am–5pm, Fri 9am–4pm. The undercroft itself is normally not open to the public. Email ahead to arrange a tour of the building. | **Tip** Walk a few steps towards Barclays Bank, then look east and in the distance you should be able to see a further memorial to the Sussex Protestant Martyrs, a white stone obelisk erected on Cliffe Hill in 1901, bearing all 17 names.

106___Metal Graves, St Anne's
A family tragedy in a tranquil spot

The inscriptions on Victorian gravestones often tell whole family stories, and a group of grave markers in St Anne's graveyard is particularly intriguing. They are not made of stone, as was most common in that era, but of metal, and there are no fewer than 12 of them, lined up neatly one behind the other. They are rare survivors of iron 'leaping boards'. Iron as a material for graves and grave markers was not as such unusual, but we are much more likely to see iron crosses or flat plates.

St Anne's is one of the most important churches in Lewes, and possibly the oldest. Its origins likely lie in the 11th century and it is thought that it was a place of pilgrimage. Originally called St Mary Westout, from the 16th century it was associated with St Anne, the patron saint of wells. The oldest surviving parts, including the tower, date from the 12th century, but the church was greatly altered in the 19th century. It is remarkably large for a church on the outskirts of a small parish and sits in an elevated position above the High Street. On Lewes Bonfire Night it is one of the prime spots for watching the processions.

The 12 iron leaping boards queue up in the north-west corner of the churchyard and mark the graves of the local Medhurst family. They were well-known millwrights in Sussex and were also involved with ironworks in the area, which suggests the boards were made there, and quite possibly by the father of the children buried here. His name was Samuel Medhurst, born in 1800. He was married to Philadelphia, and between 1831 and 1846 they buried no fewer than seven of their very young children, most of them at just a few months old. Three further children made it to adulthood but also died before their parents. Philadelphia died aged 79 and Samuel survived them all, dying in 1887. One wonders who made his leaping board.

Address St Anne's Church, High Street, BN7 1RJ, +44 (0)1273 472545, stannelewes.org.uk |
Getting there 15-minute walk from Lewes Railway Station; bus 28, 29, 29B and local buses
to Pelham Arms; some free car parking weekends and evening in County Hall car park |
Hours Churchyard always open; church usually open during the day; Sun services 8am &
10am | **Tip** The church tower is topped by a gilt copper weathervane, made in 1826, in the
shape of a cockerel. It came crashing down in the Great Storm of October 1987, but was
salvaged, restored and put back in its place.

107 __ The Needlemakers
Shop and party like it's 1899

Had enough of soulless shopping centres? The Needlemakers is an idiosyncratic assortment of around 15 independent shops, workshops and suppliers in the heart of Lewes, where Harry Potter and friends would not seem out of place.

The tall, red brick building was first built around 1820 and housed Broad's Candle Factory, but was later also used as a potter's store, a builder's merchant and the surgical-needle factory from which its name derives. The last batch of candles was produced here in 1908 and given to Lewes Museum. The building we see today dates largely from 1866 and is a splendid example of a multi-purpose Victorian industrial building, complete with the brick-lined well in the basement that once provided the water for the factory's steam power.

Unappreciated in the 20th century, the building was saved from demolition in the 1970s by conservationists. In 1984 it was converted into the charming array of shops you see today, retaining many original features. You can now enjoy browsing for bric-a-brac, high-end vintage furniture and clothes, jewellery, books and more against a backdrop of cobbled floors, wooden beams and old stable doors. The basement is particularly intriguing, with the original well still visible (although safely covered). If you ever need an outfit for a decade-themed party, the cavernous flea market shop down here, full of good-quality vintage garments, is your place. Designers often come in search of vintage fashion magazines, advertising material and dress patterns, or the largest selection of Ladybird books in town, all neatly arranged for connoisseurs of mid-20th-century print culture.

On the ground floor, a fully licensed café provides fresh plant-based food made on site, serving as a gentle centre point for the Needlemakers, a place for people to pass through, meet, talk, and wind down. It also hosts group events and parties.

Address West Street, BN7 2NZ, www.needlemakers.co.uk | **Getting there** 10-minute walk from Lewes Railway Station; bus 28, 29, 29B to Lewes High Street | **Hours** Most shops and café Mon–Fri 9–5pm, Sat 10–5pm, Sun 11–4pm | **Tip** Around the corner in Fisher Street is the Market Gate, built in 1792. Here hangs the town bell, St Gabriel, cast in 1544 and until 1761 housed in the now demolished St Nicholas Church. There is also a mural of Thomas Paine (see ch. 96), painted in 1994 by local artist Julian Bell.

108 Pells Pool
The poetry of swimming

Lewes is home to the UK's oldest freshwater outdoor public swimming pool. Built near the site of an old paper mill, for which the nearby Pells Lake (or 'Duck Pond') was created, it was financed by public subscription and opened in 1860 as part of the first town park here. Initially there were two pools, screened by a flint wall: a 'Subscription Pool' for the general public, and a larger 'Free Bath', where local workers could swim or wash without charge. The pools quickly became a popular social hub. In winter they served as ice-skating rinks, and during World War II they were used for military training.

With improvements in domestic sanitation after the war, the demand for free bathing waned. Pells Pool only narrowly escaped demolition, and was renovated and modified in 1950. The Free Pool was turned into a large tree-lined lawn, where you now have to fight for towel space on a hot day, but the original 46x23-metre Subscription Pool remains, joined by a paddling pool, a sun terrace and reassuringly vintage-looking kiosks selling tickets, ice-cream, drinks and snacks. Pells Pool is not for the faint-hearted: the pool is spring-fed and heated only by sunlight, so if you are a connoisseur of early season dips in cold water then this is your place.

At the end of the 20th century, the pool came under threat once again, but the council intervened. Since 2001 it has been run by the Pells Pool Community Association, and has become much more than swimming baths, with many events throughout the season, including midsummer night's concerts. There have been writers-in-residence for several years now, and people are encouraged to bring their poems and stories about swimming. An anthology about outdoor swimming, *Watermarks*, was published by Pells Pool and a local literary press in 2017, and there is even a small swimming pool library. You won't find a more poetic pool in the country.

Address Brook Street, Lewes, East Sussex, BN7 2BA, +44 (0)1273 472334, www.pellspool.org.uk, thepellspool@yahoo.co.uk | Getting there 15-minute walk from Lewes Railway Station; bus 28, 29, 29B, 29X to Lewes Bus Station or Lewes Waitrose | Hours Daily, mid-May–mid-Sept Mon–Fri 7am–7pm, Sat & Sun noon–7pm during May, 10am–7pm from June onwards. Pells Pool can also be hired for private events. | Tip Just outside the entrance is the L-shaped Pells Lake. This is an ideal spot for a short stroll. For a longer walk along water continue north for a few minutes until you reach the River Ouse.

109 Pipe Passage

Unsuitable for Woolf, but undeniably pretty

Pipe Passage is one of the narrowest alleys of Lewes, and roughly follows the western edge of the castle mound's footprint and the medieval town wall. It may have been the sentry walk along the castle walls, so you could imagine Norman soldiers standing watch here, protecting the town. If coming from the High Street, peep through fences and borders to your right and you will see the castle soaring up, with gardens nestling at the bottom.

At its High Street end, Pipe Passage is flanked by the attractive red-and-yellow-brick Freemason's Hall, rebuilt in 1868, and the Tom Paine Printing Press shop with its entertaining window displays, where you learn that Lewes is the 'centre of the cosmos' (not just the world!). This is run by Peter Chasseaud, who set up a working 18th-century-style wooden common press here in 2009. The press, a development of Gutenberg's 1455 model, was made in Lewes from oak and metal. It prints local artists' and writers' works, and is used for public demonstrations and courses as well. The shop also serves as gallery space for work by contemporary printmakers.

In Pipe Passage itself you will see on your left the remains of a Victorian kiln, where clay pipes were once made. Lewes had a thriving clay pipe industry and many Lewesians dig up broken pipes in their gardens. The production of these gave the passage its name. Further along are many attractive older cottages, but one stands out for its shape: the Round House.

This is the smock, or base, of a windmill, built by public subscription in 1801. It ceased working in 1819 and has long been a private house. A stone plaque tells the story of it briefly being owned by the writer Virginia Woolf. She bought it on a whim in 1919 for £300, but husband Leonard thought it was unsuitable, and they immediately put it back on the market, settling in the nearby village of Rodmell instead.

Address Next to The Tom Paine Printing Press & Press Gallery, 151 High Street, BN7 1XU | **Getting there** 15-minute walk from Lewes Railway Station; bus 28, 29, 29B to Lewes High Street then a 5-minute walk | **Hours** Always accessible. For Tom Paine Press see www.tompaineprintingpress.com. | **Tip** At the end of Pipe Passage you will reach New Road. Turn sharp right and continue up Castle Lane, at the end of which you will find one of the best viewpoints in Lewes. From here you can look north towards London and over the Paddock and Baxter's Field, Lewes' green lungs.

110 The Runaway Café

Friendly conversations with staff and strangers

If you have always had a soft spot for David Lean's classic 1945 film *Brief Encounter*, then this traditional station buffet is your place. The Runaway is a rare survivor of a family-run, no-nonsense station café. Once a staple on British railway platforms, station buffets have almost all been replaced with soulless coffee chains. Not so in Lewes. The Runaway has fought off almost as many attempts at being replaced as it has served its legendary bacon sandwiches to famous customers, including Princess Diana.

For the tired morning commuter to London there is no better refuge than this warm and inviting place offering homemade sandwiches, breakfast made to order, and coffee and tea served in proper cups and saucers. It is not old-fashioned in the old-fashioned sense – you can have a latte with soya milk if you want, ask for the Wi-Fi code and charge your phone here – but there is a gentleness about it that is rare in this fast, modern world. Classical music plays in the background, and there is a table reserved for strangers who would like to speak to others. No wonder, then, that the Runaway has become a forum for lively conversation, banter and debate, often instigated by the owner herself, Jackie Elsey, who has been running it since the 1980s.

Staff are famously friendly, and great care is given to the food and drink, much of which is sourced locally. The tea is proper leaf tea, specially blended for the chalky Sussex water. The rail companies wanted to mess with the Runaway a few years ago and replace it with a coffee chain. Unsurprisingly, Lewesians rallied behind their beloved commuter haven. Petitions were signed, and supporters threatened to boycott the coffee chain taking over the café.

The chain in question and the rail company bosses admitted defeat, and the Runaway remained in place, hopefully for many years to come.

Address Platform 2, Lewes Railway Station, Station Road, BN7 2UP, +44 (0)1273 473919, www.the-runaway.co.uk, info@the-runaway.co.uk | Hours Mon–Fri 5.10am–6.50pm, Sat 7.10am–5.50pm, Sun 8.10am–5.20pm | Tip From platform 2 you get a good view of how Lewes is nestled in the Ouse valley, with the chalk cliffs in the east and the castle ruin sitting high on the mound in the north-west. At the very end of the platform is the entrance to the railway tunnel that runs under part of the old town.

111 Southover Grange Gardens

Lewes Priory recycled

At the foot of the 'twittens' (alleyways) that run down from Lewes High Street is an oasis you may miss if you rush from the railway station to the Castle or Cliffe High Street. If you haven't broken an ankle on Keere Street's cobbles (see ch. 99), ahead of you on the next corner you'll see Southover Grange, an elegant Tudor house built in 1572 for William Newton. Do its stones look strangely out of proportion to you? They were sourced from the demolished medieval priory just a few hundred metres south (see ch. 103). The building has an interesting history and has recently been attractively refurbished. Now owned by Lewes Council, it houses the Register Office and has become one of the most popular places in Sussex to get married.

This is partly because the Grange has another great asset: exquisite south-facing gardens, abundant with colour almost all year round. The Winterbourne stream runs through it, dormant in the summer but bursting into life in winter or after heavy rain. Formal ornamental flower beds lie on the west side of the garden, while the east end features a wild area of primroses, wild strawberries and cowslips. There are magnolia and mulberry trees, as well as the country's oldest tulip tree. Thought to have been planted in 1720, it is propped up and slowly dying a beautiful death. An inscribed stone tablet commemorates a visit from the very young Queen Elizabeth II in 1951, during which she planted several new trees. Picturesque priory stone walls make the perfect backdrop for wedding pictures, and one often sees wedding parties tumbling out of the Grange to gather and pose in the gardens.

Have a wander yourself and look for sculptures by local artists John Skelton and Hamish Black, or the tranquil knot garden, created in 2004. If you haven't brought a picnic, a delightful small café operates from a small window in the north wing of the Grange.

Address Southover Road, BN7 1TP | **Getting there** 5-minute walk from Lewes Railway Station; bus 28, 29, 29B to Lewes High Street | **Hours** Daily 8.30am–dusk or 9pm, whichever is earlier | **Tip** The north wing is also the headquarters, shop and gallery of The Sussex Guild, a group of designers and makers of contemporary and traditional crafts, including ceramics and jewellery, founded in 1968 (+44 (0)1273 479565, www.thesussexguild.co.uk).

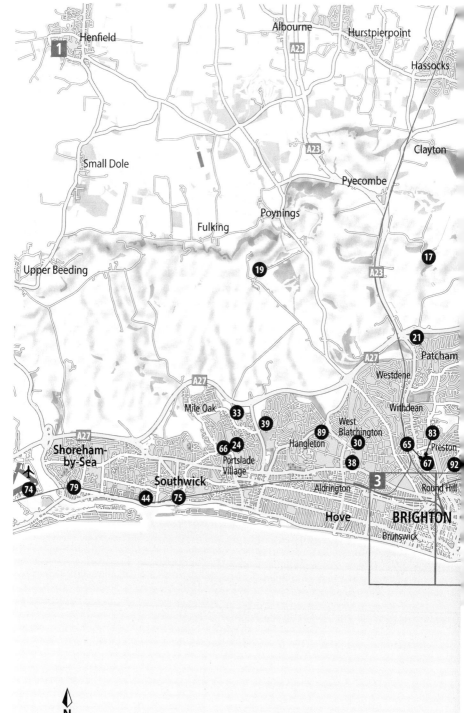

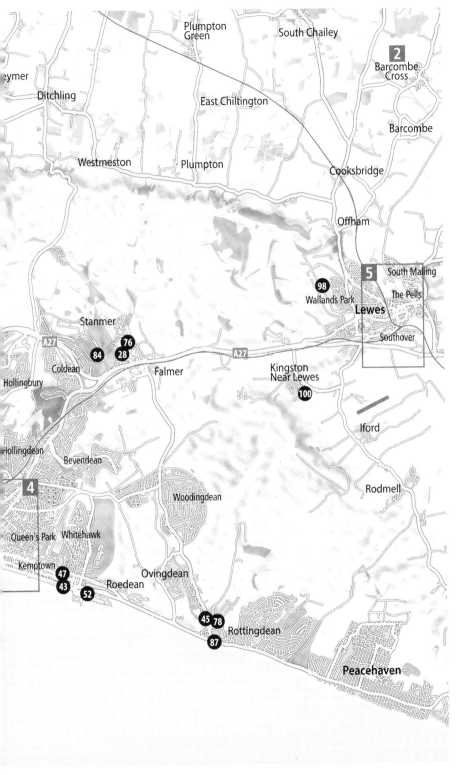

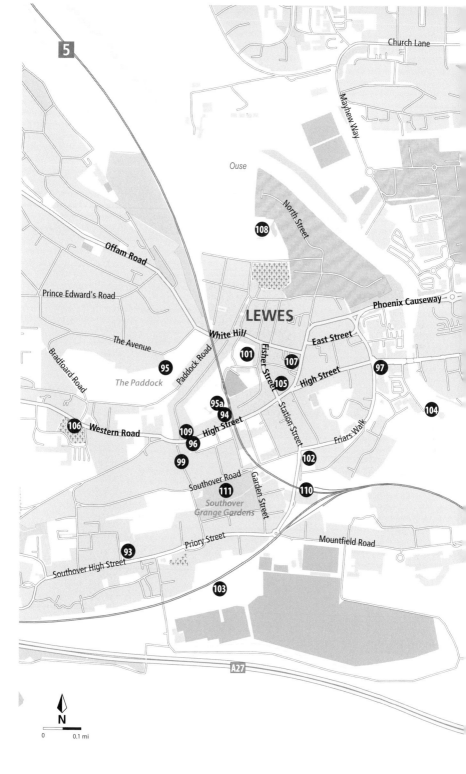

Katherine Bebo, Oliver Smith
**111 Places in Bournemouth
That You Shouldn't Miss**
ISBN 978-3-7408- 1166-2

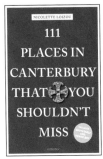

Nicolette Loizou
**111 Places in Canterbury
That You Shouldn't Miss**
ISBN 978-3-7408-0899-0

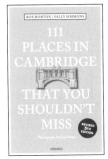

Rosalind Horton,
Sally Simmons, Guy Snape
**111 Places in Cambridge
That You Shouldn't Miss**
ISBN 978-3-7408-0147-2

John Sykes, Birgit Weber
**111 Places in London
That You Shouldn't Miss**
ISBN 978-3-7408-1168-6

Ed Glinert, Marc Zakian
**111 Places in London's
East End That You
Shouldn't Miss**
ISBN 978-3-7408-0752-8

Solange Berchemin,
Martin Dunford, Karin Tearle
**111 Places in Greenwich
That You Shouldn't Miss**
ISBN 978-3-7408-1107-5

Solange Berchemin
**111 Places in the Lake District
That You Shouldn't Miss**
ISBN 978-3-7408-0378-0

Rob Ganley, Ian Williams
**111 Places in Coventry
That You Shouldn't Miss**
ISBN 978-3-7408-1044-3

Martin Booth, Barbara Evripidou
**111 Places in Bristol
That You Shouldn't Miss**
ISBN 978-3-7408-1612-4

A note on transport

The city of Brighton & Hove is densely populated, with a pattern of narrow streets in the centre. There is very little street parking available, and public car parks are expensive. It is highly advisable to visit via public transport. Brighton main railway station is a five-minute walk from the centre and has rail links to London, the east coast (including Lewes) and the west coast (including Portslade and Shoreham). Parking in Lewes is marginally easier, but the town easily becomes clogged with traffic, so cars are best avoided. The regional bus network is large and serves the entire area covered in the book, with more than 60 bus lines and several bus companies operating, too many to list individually for each place in this book. For information on bus services visit www.buses.co.uk, for rail services www.southernrailway.com or www.nationalrail.co.uk. For tickets and advice on local travel by bus, coach or train visit 1 Stop Travel, 26 North St, Brighton, BN1 1EB.

Acknowledgements

There are many people I would like to thank for supporting me in writing this book. First of all the wonderful and supportive team at Emons, especially Laura Olk and Alison Jean Lester. It has been such a privilege and pleasure working with you. Thanks are due to the many friends and colleagues who suggested places to include and provided me with vital information, among them Tracy Anderson, Paul Couchman, Jackie Jones, Tamsin Mastoris, Ann Smith and Rob Stephenson. There are just too many to mention here, but all your help was appreciated. Special thanks to David Beevers, who recommended me as an author, Franky Bulmer for first introducing me to the beauty of England, Clive Boursnell, Rose Jones, Carlotta Luke, Strat Mastoris, as well as several of the '111 Places' for generously providing some of the photographs, and Steve Pavey, who drove me around in his trusted Mini Cooper and tested many a café and pub with me. Big thanks are due to my family, Jeremy and Flora, who had to spend many weekends and evenings without me. Lastly, I want to thank everyone in Sussex, my chosen home since 1997, who made me feel welcome here and gave me opportunities.

Alexandra Loske is an art historian and curator with a particular interest in late eighteenth and early nineteenth century European art and architecture. She has been working at the University of Sussex since 1999 and at the Royal Pavilion in Brighton since 2008. She has curated a number of exhibition and displays, including ones on Regency Colour, exotic and non-native animals, local history and the life and times of Jane Austen. She has lectured and published widely on colour history and related topics, appeared as an art historian on many TV and radio programmes, has organised conferences and writes regularly for local and national magazines, as well as the official Brighton Museums blog.